LOST
CEDAR RAPIDS

LOST
CEDAR RAPIDS

PETER D. LOONEY

THE
History
PRESS

Published by The History Press
Charleston, SC
www.historypress.com

Front cover: The BCR&N and Rock Island Depot, circa 1910, located on First Avenue in what is known today as the Skogman parking lot. *Courtesy of the History Center, Linn County Historical Society.*

First published 2020

Manufactured in the United States

ISBN 9781467140652

Library of Congress Control Number: 2020934340

This book is dedicated to my sweet and saintly wife, Julie Beth Looney, my partner for more than forty-five years on this incredibly fun ride on planet Earth, and to our awesome daughters, Heidi and Jennifer, who continuously bring joy to our lives.

CONTENTS

CONTENTS

PREFACE

I f we divide the state of Iowa into geographic thirds: western Iowa is good, flat, black farmland with some lengthy distance between the towns; central Iowa is the home of our state capital, Des Moines; and eastern Iowa borders the Mississippi River and offers the cities of Cedar Rapids, Waterloo, Iowa City, Dubuque, Davenport and Burlington.

I grew up in a big family on a tiny farm near the small town of Solon, located between Cedar Rapids and Iowa City. Our landlord's house was an old stagecoach stop that was built in the 1850s, situated on Dillons Furrow, later known as the Old Military Road, and now known as Highway 1. My life was all about school, church, farmwork and family—balanced with laughter, love, books, music, good food and homemade fun.

My interest in "historical things" began at an early age. I loved looking at old photos. My mother was always looking for additions to her collections of fossils and arrowheads. Every summer, the folks would pack the eight of us and our picnic and camping gear into the car and head out across the country to visit such places as Yellowstone, Gettysburg and the Alamo, always making time to stop by tourist attractions like the world's largest ball of mud à la the movie *National Lampoon's Vacation*.

My earliest memories include car rides with the family peering out of the windows and seeing rural Iowa's old buildings as we passed by. Solon had its share of old, interesting buildings, and nearby was the one-horse town of Sutliff, which was right across the Cedar River from our grandpa's farm. I treasure the memory of driving Grandpa's old John Deere tractor across the rickety one-lane Sutliff bridge and going into the old general store to warm up.

Ghost towns always intrigued me. The long-gone town of Ivanhoe, where Highway 1 crosses the Cedar, was nothing but a burned-out foundation of a tavern overgrown with weeds and trees on the south side and just a few buildings, cabins and a sand pit on the north side. This was a *town*?

We'd make the occasional special trip into Cedar Rapids. Picture a skinny little kid on an older sister's lap, nose pressed up against the car window and gazing in wonder at the tall buildings. And look at all these people—there must be hundreds of them.

Later, as an adult living in Cedar Rapids with my own family, I'd wonder about all the landmarks I kept hearing about—the Majestic, the Allison, the Montrose, the Masonic Temple, the Union Depot, Star Wagon—where had they been? Where did they go? What's there now?

That island in the middle of the river in the heart of downtown—why are there buildings on it? Was there really a roller coaster on it at one point? Yes! I'd hear about this outdoor movie theater, only it was a walk-in and not a drive-in. And I'd hear people talk about all these other grand old theaters, crazy dance halls, magnificent hotels, four different amusement parks and five different racetracks. Where were they, and when were they there and where did they go?

So, I started collecting old pictures that I'd come across in newspapers, magazines, books and, eventually, on the internet. I'd study them with a magnifying glass. I made lists of those old places, their addresses, the years they were there, what was there before them and what is there now. I followed this with hundreds and hundreds of hours probing and researching old newspapers, phone books and city directories to find accurate dates of existence and operation—all resulting in this book.

Cedar Rapids has so many lost landmarks and interesting places, and some of them are still around. There are so many landmarks that this book is barely scratching the surface. Yet, here it is.

ACKNOWLEDGEMENTS

Thanks, Mother!

Maxine Looney passed away in 2017 at the age of ninety-four. She taught me to love reading and writing. She wrote poetry, columns for the *Solon Economist* and articles about local history. She also gave talks on fossils and other geological wonders. She was an inspiration to me and countless others. She will be best remembered as a lifelong Sunday school teacher. She had pretty much the entire Bible memorized and loved sharing stories and their meanings with others. I give her full credit for anything I write that might be interesting. For everything else, you can blame me.

Thanks, Rick!

Rick Sampson became a friend of mine just a few years ago. I first heard his voice on AM radio, way back, broadcasting from local studios and sharing good information with the citizens of Cedar Rapids and eastern Iowa. Then he and I officially met on a wildly popular Facebook page called Cedar Rapids History. Rick thought my collections of local historical facts would interest fellow history buffs, and he routinely borrows my lists and shares them. Let it be known that Rick has the unusual distinction of posting only accurate information on the World Wide Web.

Thanks, Carly!

Carly Weber was my brilliant editor at the *Cedar Rapids Gazette*. One of her projects was the excellent weekly entertainment magazine, the *Hoopla*.

She contracted me to provide interviews and articles about local musicians and bands and, every now and then, a national act passing through the area. Initially, she had half a dozen music contributors, but as they wandered away, I was the only one left. I ended up profiling just over one hundred musicians and bands. I'm pleased that Carly dedicated so much print space to the local music scene. I'm honored to have been part of it, and Carly and I remain friends to this day.

Thanks, Susan!

Susan O'Shaughnessy is my sister. The six Looney kids included Joyce, Frankie, Tim, David, Susan and me. Oh, I have superb siblings—all are thoughtful, kind, funny, musical and extremely and unusually intelligent. I'm not sure what happened to me, although I am somewhat musical. But I digress. Susan became aware that this book needed to be written, and she offered me continual encouragement and editing improvements. And she gets the importance of history—she now resides on what we still call Grandpa's Farm out by Sutliff.

And a shout-out to my brother Tim Looney, who, after hearing me go on and on about wishing I was a writer, suggested I pick up a pen and actually write something. So, I did.

INTRODUCTION

For many years, Cedar Rapids has been proud to promote its nickname, the "City of Five Seasons." Four of the seasons are winter, spring, summer and fall. The fifth season is "the time to enjoy the other four." A flourishing center for arts and culture in eastern Iowa, the city is home to the Cedar Rapids Museum of Art, National Czech & Slovak Museum & Library, Theatre Cedar Rapids, Paramount Theatre, Orchestra Iowa, African American Museum of Iowa and Mother Mosque of America— the oldest standing purpose-built mosque in the United States. The award-winning daily newspaper, the *Cedar Rapids Gazette*, has been providing readers with good information since 1883.

A small list of some of the famous citizens who came from Cedar Rapids include actors Ashton Kutcher, Elijah Wood and Ron Livingston; musician Michael Boddicker; TV and movie star Don Defore from the '50s and '60s; star athletes Zach Johnson and Kurt Warner; former first lady Mamie Eisenhower; authors William Shirer and Ed Gorman; artists Grant Wood and Marvin Cone; photographer Carl Van Vechten; and the flying Wright brothers, Wilbur and Orville.

Less famous to the rest of world but important to the early development and growth of Cedar Rapids are men such as Greene, Bever, Ely, Daniels and Ellis, and later on, Sinclair, Stuart, Coe, Douglas, Smulekoff, Armstrong and Hall—more about them later.

Founded in 1838 and incorporated in 1849, Cedar Rapids is the seventh-oldest city in Iowa. Iowa state senators proudly offered the following recognition of Iowa's second-largest city on its 150th anniversary:

IOWA SENATE JOURNAL for THURSDAY, APRIL 22, 1999
On motion of Senator Mary Lundby, a Senate Resolution honoring the City of Cedar Rapids on its sesquicentennial year was taken up for consideration.
SENATE RESOLUTION NO. 15 BY HORN, DVORSKY, MCKEAN, AND LUNDBY
A Resolution honoring the City of Cedar Rapids on its sesquicentennial year.
WHEREAS, the City of Cedar Rapids was incorporated in 1849 and has since evolved as one of the finest cities in America; and
WHEREAS, 1999 marks the sesquicentennial anniversary year of the City of Cedar Rapids; and
WHEREAS, the City of Cedar Rapids has chosen its sesquicentennial anniversary to celebrate its rich cultural, educational, industrial, and civic history; and
WHEREAS, the City of Cedar Rapids has chosen a different celebration theme for each month of 1999:
January—kickoff, February—diversity, March—volunteers, April—learning, May—architecture, June—history, July—freedom, August—neighborhoods, September—labor, October—business, November—recreation, and December—looking forward for another 150 years;
NOW THEREFORE, BE IT RESOLVED BY THE SENATE, that the Senate recognizes and extends its congratulations to the City of Cedar Rapids on its sesquicentennial anniversary year and for its 150 years of service to its citizens and to the State of Iowa.
BE IT FURTHER RESOLVED, that an official copy of this Resolution be prepared and presented to the Honorable Lee R. Clancey, Mayor of the City of Cedar Rapids.
Senator Lundby moved the adoption of Senate Resolution 15, which motion prevailed by a voice vote:
Ayes, 49
Nays, none
Absent, 1

The sixty-foot-tall Tree of Five Seasons was erected in 1996 near the commonly accepted site where Osgood Shepherd built his log cabin on the east bank of the river. According to the designer of the original Five Seasons slogan, "Life is the sum of all the seasons with which it is filled, growing, learning, working, enjoying.... Here we have the time to live. The important things are only minutes away, and we spend our time doing, not going." A great reminder to our citizens and a nice welcome to travelers. *Photo by Peter D. Looney.*

PRE-HISTORY

For more than twelve thousand years, Native American societies lived in harmony with the land here in the Father of Water's basin. The earliest Iowans were Woodland Paleo-Indians—hunters and foragers who eventually settled into villages, growing vegetables, fruits and nuts and hunting bison, elk and deer. Until a few centuries ago, the range of the Ioway tribes covered most of this area. As the Plains Indians moved and migrated, gradually, the Sioux Nation extended their range from the Dakotas into Iowa. Most recently, what is now eastern Iowa was home to the Meskwaki/Fox and the Sac/Sauk tribes.

When European Americans began spreading out across the country, explorers and adventurers and families heading west followed paths and trails, leading to the best places to cross rivers. One such place was right here. The river was wide, the water was low and there were rapids between the banks, which were lined with red cedar trees. The river bottom was rocky and solid, making this an ideal place to ford.

In wintertime, when the river froze, travelers could cross as they pleased. But when the water was flowing, there was always some risk. At this particular spot, there happened to be a large wooded island in the center of the river, and just to its north was a big partially submerged rock called the Fording Rock. If the bulk of the rock was showing, the river level was low, and it was safe to cross. But if very little of the rock was showing, the river was high, and travelers had to wait for the water to recede. The flow of the river has since been manipulated by man and dams, but the Fording Rock is still visible today when the river is low.

An enterprising frontiersman and trapper, Osgood Shepherd, arrived in 1837 and built a log cabin on the bank of the east side of the river. Rumors abound that Osgood Shepherd was a thief and hid stolen horses on the island. There is no documentation to back up these stories, but people love rumors and gossip, and the stories prevail today.

It is true that Mr. Shepherd was the first white American settler in the area, and he allowed travelers to stop and stay at his cabin as they waited for a safe time to cross the river. He eventually expanded his cabin into an inn. Shortly after Osgood's arrival, other travelers also decided that this looked like a good place to stop and live. A town was platted on the east side in 1838, and early settler William Stone named the town Columbus. In 1841, it was resurveyed by Nicholas Brown, who renamed it Rapids City. The final and majestic name of Cedar Rapids was designated in 1849 during the town's incorporation to honor the cedar trees and the tumbling rapids.

A colorful description of the process of property acquisition comes from A.J. Mallahan, the publisher of the 1883 city directory: "It was the practice of the generous founders of Cedar Rapids, in those days—a practice long since abandoned by their descendants—to give a building lot to every passenger who saw fit to accept one and take out his deed. Ah, the good old days of '42 and '43."

Before long, David W. King had also arrived, and he bought land on the other side of the river and platted the westside town of Kingston. It was briefly called West Cedar Rapids before finally becoming part of Cedar Rapids. The sports stadium on the hill is still proudly named Kingston

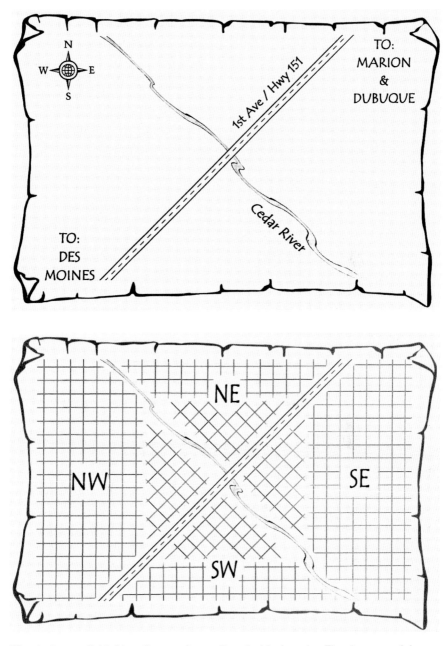

The city is now divided into four quadrants aligned with zip codes. First Avenue and the Cedar River are perpendicular to each other and tend to run diagonally instead of along the cardinal directions. First Avenue divides the north and south sides of the city, while the river divides east and west. *Artwork by Peter D. Looney.*

Stadium. Daniel Ellis was another early westside settler, and today, the northern part of his property is the spacious and beautiful Ellis Park.

The city has since been divided into four quadrants—Northeast, Southeast, Northwest and Southwest—and aligned with separate zip codes. First Avenue and the Cedar River are perpendicular to each other and tend to run diagonally instead of along the cardinal directions. It was determined early on that First Avenue divides the north and south sides of the city, while the river divides east and west.

When the city's streets were originally named, they were given colorful names, such as Iowa, Eagle, Park and Commercial, or they were named after presidents or local city leaders. But in 1882, the naming structure changed, and the streets were renamed with a numbering system and a few letters. So, if you're ever looking at an old city map or browsing an old newspaper or city directory, the following is the street name conversion chart, courtesy of the *Cedar Rapids Times*, August 24, 1882. This list refers to streets on the east side of the river.

First Avenue—Iowa Avenue
Second Avenue—Eagle Street
Third Avenue—Park or Market Avenue
Fourth Avenue—Franklin Avenue
Fifth Avenue—Greene Street
Sixth Avenue—Brown Street
Seventh Avenue—Daniels Street
Eighth Avenue—Sanford Street
Ninth Avenue—Carpenter Street
Tenth Avenue—Legare Street
Eleventh Avenue—Weare Street
Twelfth Avenue—Shearer Street
Thirteenth Avenue—Lewis Street
Fourteenth Avenue—James or May Street
A Avenue—Linn Street
B Avenue—Benton Street
C Avenue—Johnson Street
D Avenue—Ely Street
First Street—Commercial Street
Second Street—Washington Street
Third Street—Adams Street
Fourth Street—Jefferson / railway tracks

Fifth Street—Madison Street
Sixth Street—Monroe Street
Seventh Street—Jackson Street
Eighth Street—Van Buren Street
Ninth Street—Mills Street
Tenth Street—Martha Street
Eleventh Street—Harrison Street
Twelfth Street—Williams or Tyler Street
Thirteenth Street—Polk Street
Fourteenth Street—Coe Street

Settlers continued to arrive, more homes were built and businesses multiplied. Cedar Rapids quickly became the largest city in eastern Iowa and, in 2020, is home to 140,000 folks. If you add the connected cities of Marion and Hiawatha, it can boast a population of more than 250,000 citizens. And they all need places to live, work, shop and be entertained. Fortunately, they came to the right place.

PART I

ENTERTAINMENT

1
THEATERS

I had no idea of the character. But the moment I was dressed, the clothes and the make-up made me feel the person he was. I began to know him, and by the time I walked onto the stage he was fully born.
—Charlie Chaplin

Why have some people always needed to act out skits and plays while others prefer to sit and watch and clap with delight? Comedies, tragedies, musical performances—we love to be entertained. Although there's no record of it, even in the earliest days of Cedar Rapids, after the day's work was done and the children were fed, one end of a room would be cleared, becoming the stage, and shows would be performed.

Occasionally, an existing building was repurposed to become a temporary theater, but eventually, permanent sites were chosen, and social halls and auditoriums were built. As early Cedar Rapids quickly became the center of the area's social activity, traveling entertainers, speakers and musicians began to make regular stops in town. Most of the theaters were storefronts that were hurriedly remodeled into theaters and had relatively short life spans, but several were magnificent venues and true landmarks, such as Greene's, the Majestic, the World, the Paramount and the Iowa.

An evening at the theater was a wonderful, and sometimes magical, thing. In 1928, the *Cedar Rapids Republican* promoted a weeklong performance offered at the Majestic Theater, stating, "Mysterious Smith Co. presents *The Temple of Mystery*, with Mme Olga, the Worlds Famous Mind Reader and Psychic Marvel. A Complete Production of Sensational Illusions." How could you even consider not paying the thirty-five-, fifty- or seventy-five-cent admission fee and miss this show?

The following are profiles of the thirty-nine theaters that have provided Cedar Rapids citizens with all kinds of magical entertainment over the last 156 years—some indoors, some outdoors, some highbrow and some a little less sophisticated. Of these, five theaters remain active today.

UNION OPERA HOUSE

In 1862, at the northwest corner of First Avenue NE and Second Street, a narrow, four-story building called the Union Block was built. Retail storefronts, a jewelry store and the Union Bank were on the first floor, offices were on the second floor, more offices and the Masonic Scottish Rite social hall were on the third floor, and the fourth floor was an auditorium, referred to as the Union Opera House. Plays, music, lectures, graduation ceremonies, talent shows, book readings and other performances were routinely offered.

Decades later, in the 1950s, the building was covered with white aluminum panels and was home to the Morris Plan, but it was torn down in 1969. The Brenton Bank building that replaced it was designed with a unique rust-colored metal exterior and still stands today, housing a Wells Fargo bank.

GREENE'S OPERA HOUSE

Judge George Greene, an early civic leader, decided a proper theater was needed, so next door to the Union Block, he built the stately Greene's Opera House at 113 Second Street NE. Completed in 1880, it was a magnificent four-story building taken up entirely by a massive main floor theater and three floors of balconies.

The 1883 Cedar Rapids City Directory stated, "The building has a 60 feet front, with a depth of 140 feet. The walls are of pressed brick, with stone and black brick trimmings, giving it a neat and imposing appearance. The decorations are brilliant, and in excellent taste. The stage is 40 x 60 feet, elaborately and expensively furnished with scenery, etc. It is seated with the

Greene's Opera House was built next door to the Union Block in 1880, with seating for 1,600. *Courtesy of the History Center, Linn County Historical Society.*

best folding opera chairs for an audience of 1,800 to 2,000. Altogether it is one of the finest opera houses west of Chicago."

This fine venue made it easy to attract not only the best entertainers in the nation but also the best of the world's entertainers as they traveled the United States. Actual operas were rarely offered, but "opera house" sounded more distinguished than "theater."

Around the turn of the century, traveling vaudeville troupes were the main attraction. But by 1920, increased competition from smaller venues and moving picture shows had reduced audiences to the point that a decision was made to discontinue live performances. Greene's Opera House closed, and Greene's Cinema House opened. Movies were shown here from 1922 until closing in 1934. By then, the building had become terribly neglected and rundown. A large door was cut into the front, and the building became the City Parking Garage, used mostly by downtown workers and guests of the neighboring Roosevelt Hotel. It served that purpose well into the '60s. For a few more years, the formerly elegant theater building was used for auto parts storage and then the entire enterprise was demolished in 1969.

PEOPLES THEATER

In 1906, a block to the west of Greene's, backing up to the river at 137 First Street NE, the Peoples Theater was built next door to the city's newest social hall, the Auditorium. A small building, this venue featured vaudeville acts and other live stage performances. The house prospered under the successful management of Victor Hugo Klassens, offering less than notable attractions—plays, singers, comedians, vaudeville acts and Power's Cameragraph (movies). Peoples Theater remained an entertainment venue until 1913. After that, the building was repurposed many times and was finally torn down in the '60s.

DELPHUS/A-MUSE-U/CRYSTAL/RIALTO/TOWN THEATER

As train traffic on the Fourth Street corridor increased, the heart of downtown shifted closer to that area. At 310 First Avenue NE, a small, one-and-a-half-story wood frame store was converted into a theater called the Delphus. It opened in 1906 and was the first theater in town to feature moving pictures. Renamed four times, it became the A-Muse-U Theatre in 1912, was rebuilt and operated as the Crystal Theater from 1913 to 1923, the Rialto Theater from 1923 to 1948 and the Town Theater from 1948 to 1954. It eventually fell to the wrecking ball and was a parking lot for twenty years before becoming part of the Five Seasons Center in the '70s. That was remodeled and rebuilt in the 2000s and is now called the US Cellular Center.

BIJOU/LYRIC/GRAND THEATER

The Grand Hotel on First Avenue decided it, too, should offer movies and remodeled its street-level storefront on the east end of the hotel, at 306 First Avenue NE, which happened to be nearly next door to the Delphus. Opening in 1906, it began service to the public as the Bijou Theater, becoming the Lyric Theater in 1907. In 1920, it was renamed the Grand Theater and stayed in use until the early 1930s. The entire Grand Hotel building was torn down in 1951.

MAJESTIC THEATRE

Situated where part of the US Cellular Convention Center sits today, at the intersection of Third Street and A Avenue NE, was the Jim Block, an office building erected in 1900. Several years later, the owners recognized the city's need for a new theater and added a second building directly behind it, along A Avenue.

The Majestic Theatre opened in 1908. The front office building, with an address of 129 Third Street NE, provided the entrance with a portico and lobby, with a long hallway and stairs leading up to various levels of the theater. As announced in the May 2, 1908 edition of the *Gazette*, "the theater was designed by Rapp of Chicago, who make a specialty of theater architecture, and who have the charge of remodeling and construction of new theaters for the Western Vaudeville Managers Association. They are among the best theater architects in the country."

The Majestic's owners then hired Victor Hugo Klassens, who had been managing the Peoples Theater, as the manager. He and his wife moved into the living quarters in the theater, complete with kitchen, living room, several bedrooms and bathrooms and a maid's quarters.

The auditorium seated 1,400. Promoted as a "high-class vaudeville house," the theater offered audiences and performers alike the latest in modern conveniences, including fourteen furnished dressing rooms, lobbies on all three floors and a separate entrance to the upper balcony, where "cheap seats" were available. Ticket prices ranged from ten cents to a dollar.

Theatergoers in Cedar Rapids had a reputation for having high expectations. At one point, a sign was reportedly posted backstage in New York City's Majestic Theatre, reading, "You think you're good? Try playing Cedar Rapids!" Reinforcing that reputation was a sign posted backstage at the Cedar Rapids Majestic, stating, "Don't send out your laundry until we've seen your act!"

In 1921, the theater added movies, but vaudeville remained the featured presentation. Patriotic acts such as John Philip Sousa's band were often booked for engagements. Other headliners included popular stars such as Bob Hope, Jack Benny, George Burns and Gracie Allen.

During the lifetime of the theater, the Majestic had the misfortune of experiencing a string of disasters. In 1913, structural deficiencies required the closing of the theater for substantial remodeling. The theater reopened after repairs were made, but in 1915, a tank filled with six thousand gallons of water for the "Six Diving Nymphs" burst on stage during a

Top: Seating on the Majestic's main floor and two balconies allowed for 1,400 patrons. *Author's collection.*

Bottom: The Majestic, built in 1908, was Cedar Rapids' premier vaudeville theater. *Author's collection.*

performance, flooding and damaging the main floor. Later in 1915, the roof over the stage collapsed, destroying the lighting system, scenery, box seats and proscenium arch. After a $30,000 refurbishing job and several months, the Majestic reopened.

Problems continued. The lack of air conditioning forced it to close during the summers. Then, with the introduction of talking motion pictures, vaudeville's popularity began fading, and the crowds seriously decreased. New management was brought in, but by then, the theater was struggling financially. It closed permanently in 1933, a victim of the depression, the waning of vaudeville and competition from new venues. The owners were deeply in debt.

In 1934, the theater burned in a suspicious blaze. The origins of the fire were never discovered. The following year, the burned-out structure was declared a hazard and was demolished.

AIRDOME

The Airdome was an outdoor theater at 301 Third Street NE, located in a large fenced-in and gated lot, which eventually became part of the Quaker Oats property. Ads promoted one thousand seats, which were neatly lined up folding chairs and bleachers. It operated during the summers from 1908 to 1912, offering plays, vaudeville and movies. You could see two movies for one dime. Even the advertising promoted the value: "$1 SHOWS FOR 10¢." The risk of inclement weather at outdoor shows was also addressed on the posters: "ON STORMY NIGHTS, SHOWS WILL BE HELD AT GREENE'S."

The Airdome outdoor entertainment venue. *Author's collection.*

(THE ORIGINAL) PALACE THEATER

A small building located on First Avenue between First and Second Streets NE was squeezed in between the Masonic Temple/ORC&B building and the Union Block/Morris Plan/Baranchanu's buildings. It had been home to several businesses before the turn of the twentieth century, including serving as one of the many locations of the Sunshine Mission. When the mission relocated to better serve the needs of the homeless and underprivileged, the building was converted to a movie theater.

The four-hundred-seat Palace Theatre opened for business in May 1908, as the *Gazette* noted, "Proprietors of the new Palace Theatre in downtown Cedar Rapids said the facility would open this week. Located in the former Sunshine Mission building, the owners promised to show only high-class moving pictures and illustrated songs for five cents admission." This theater had a short life span, as it was never mentioned again in any subsequent newspaper or city directory.

PALACE THEATER

A new Palace Theatre opened in 1912 at 310 Second Avenue SE and was owned by Mike Ford, a local businessman in the asphalt and paving industry. The theater seated seven hundred, and music was provided by the Palace Orchestra.

The Palace had a long life span and changed management only after the first successful forty-four years. According to an article in the December 12, 1956 *Gazette*:

> *Roy Metcalfe, operator of the Times Theater, has leased the Palace Theater from the Palace Theater Company, it was announced Saturday. He takes over the theater immediately, having acquired it on a long-term lease. He will also continue to operate the Times. The Palace is a return-movie theater. The Palace building continues to be the property of the heirs of A.J. Diebold and Mike Ford, the theater's founders. The families have operated the theater almost continuously. William J. McGuire has managed it for many years. Mr. Metcalfe has been in show business for 26 years and in Cedar Rapids for 10 years. His wife assists him in theater operation. Metcalfe said Saturday that he plans to remodel the Palace.*

Incidentally, the 1957 remodeling resulted in the relocation of a longtime tenant. In 1936, the Palace Barbershop had moved in, sharing the marquee and proving to be a popular place for a haircut and a shave. After moving out in 1957, the Palace Barbershop changed locations several times but finally found a permanent home in the Alliant Tower in 2009.

The Palace Theater closed in 1960, and the building was demolished a year later. In its place is the Second Avenue entrance to the US Bank parking ramp.

PRINCESS THEATRE

In the silent film era, movie theaters popped up everywhere. Usually, a struggling retail building's owner would open the interior on the ground level of the building, paint the wall at one end of the room white, procure a projector, find some chairs and announce the opening of the grand new theater. Cedar Rapids had several such theaters, and not much is known about them today, other than their opening dates. Some were certainly nicer than others. The Princess Theatre opened in 1910 at 323 Second Avenue SE (next door to what eventually became the Dragon Restaurant) and showed five-cent movies for the next seven years.

OLYMPIC/SUN/STRAND/CEDAR RAPIDS COMMUNITY THEATRE

As central European immigrants learned that Cedar Rapids offered jobs and a welcoming place to build new lives, the south edge of town became largely settled with Czech and Slovak citizens. By the turn of the century, Czechs had established homes, businesses, churches and social organizations. The first theater in that area was the Olympic Theatre, built in 1910 on the northeast corner of Third Street and Twelfth Avenue SE. Also known as the South Side Theater, it was situated right in the heart of the Bohemian district. It offered a variety of performances, but Slavic-language movies were a particularly popular attraction.

In 1936, with new owners, the Olympic was renamed the Sun. It moved away from cultural movies and now showed standard Hollywood fare. But it didn't last long under the Sun name and closed a year later.

After sitting idle, it reopened in late 1939 as the Strand. This was actually the second "Strand" in Cedar Rapids—the first one, downtown, had changed its name to the State a decade earlier. Focusing on second-run Hollywood flicks such as westerns and comedies, the new Strand continued offering movies for twelve years, until it finally closed in 1951.

Meanwhile, around town, local actors were creating their own performance traditions. In 1925, Cedar Rapids thespians founded the Little Theater group, changing the name to the Community Players in 1929. Any available stage was their place of production, and eventually, the YMCA offered a consistent location. After the group was renamed the Footlighters in 1948, Coe College offered the use of its stage for several years. But by 1955, the organization needed a home of its own, and it happily moved into the old Olympic/Strand. Now renamed the Cedar Rapids Community Theatre (CRCT), it finally had its first permanent home.

As noted on the group's website today, "since the grand opening in the former Strand Theatre back in 1955, the Cedar Rapids Community Theatre has come a long way."

That opening night, reporter Nadine Subotnik wrote in the *Gazette*, "Was done in true premiere style. A searchlight pierced the sky, floodlights shone on the theater front, and a huge birthday cake sat atop the marquee. Jack Ware, who has been on stage in past Footlighter productions, conducted sidewalk interviews. Oh, it was a gala first night."

The theater flourished. In 1969, it installed "comfortable seats and air conditioning," which allowed for an expanded production calendar. Season ticket prices grew from $6 in 1955 to "a whopping $17 in 1976." A *Gazette* review noted, "Cramped and creaky though it may be, the old theater on 3rd Street provides a choice setting for CRCT's productions."

In 1981, the theater organization relocated to the elegant Iowa Theater building downtown, where it remains today under the name Theatre Cedar Rapids.

Back on Third Street, in 1984, after a few years standing vacant, the former Olympic/Strand/CRCT building reopened as a tavern/nightclub called the Opera House Night Club, offering beverages and entertainment until 1992. After that business closed, the building was torn down in 1993. Today, the property is part of the NewBo City Market grassy plaza.

COLUMBIA THEATER

Next door to the massive Allison Hotel, the Columbia Theater opened at 313 First Avenue SE, in 1912. Directly across the street were two existing theaters, the Lyric and the Crystal. Interestingly enough, these three neighboring theaters were all converted storefronts, and all three were eventually replaced by larger entertainment venues. The Columbia was replaced by the Iowa Theater building in 1928, and the Five Seasons/US Cellular Center was built on the site of the Lyric and the Crystal in 1979.

WEST SIDE THEATRE

Cedar Rapidians living on the west side of town wanted entertainment venues too. Happily, in 1912, two movie houses opened on "their side" of the river. These two were both converted from existing storefronts, and they were right across the street from each other.

The West Side Theatre opened in 1912 in the King Building at 213 First Street SW and showed movies for seven years. It had closed by 1919, when an auto parts store took over the building, followed shortly by the Cedar Rapids Police, which used the building as its headquarters from 1923 to 1926.

FAMILY THEATRE

The Family Theatre at 212 First Street SW also opened in 1912, with very little fanfare, and the Family Theatre closed fairly quickly, also with very little fanfare.

ISIS THEATRE

The Isis Theatre, with its Egyptian-themed decorations, was owned by Clement & Sutherland and opened in late 1913. At 315 Second Avenue SE, the theater was right next to the Second Avenue post office (later MeToo/ Witwer.) The second floor of the building was the Isis Hotel. This was definitely theater row, with the Princess two doors down and the Palace right across the street.

The Isis primarily showed silent films, but its stage was regularly used as a backup to the larger Greene and Majestic venues, when their stages were overbooked. Occasionally, special acts, such Sousa and His Band, would be passing through town, and the big venues would book them for one-night engagements, conflicting with previously scheduled shows. When this happened, the regular stage show would move to the Isis Theatre for the night.

The Isis operated until the end of the silent era, closing in 1928. In 1930, it was remodeled into offices for Western Union, lasting through the '60s, followed by three decades of Paris Beauty/Capri Cosmetology. After another half a dozen years serving as various bars, the building was demolished in 2014.

PRAHA THEATER

The Praha Theater opened in 1913 at 227 Fourteenth Avenue SE, which was the busy south side intersection of Third Street and Fourteenth Avenue SE, where you could either proceed into the Sinclair packing house property or head west toward the river and Czech Village. Meaning "Prague" in the Czech language, the Praha was respectfully named for the Czech capital. But the Cedar Rapids movie operation didn't turn out to be a success and closed after only three years, in 1916.

After housing a milk depot and then various taverns over the years, the building remains today as part of Mad Modern, a vintage furnishings shop.

IDEAL THEATER

Three doors down from the Praha, toward the river, the Ideal Theater opened for business at 215 Fourteenth Avenue SE on July 4, 1914.

The *Gazette* reported, "The new Ideal Theater opened this afternoon, showing Mary Pickford in 'Caprice' before a large crowd. F.J. Smid, the owner, has made arrangements with the Mutual Service and the Famous Players. The theater is equipped with a mirror screen, Powers Cameograph machine, and all the latest equipment. The theater has a capacity of 500 and is equipped with eight ventilators, ensuring pure air at all times."

The theater closed in 1917 during the first World War, but after a two-year hiatus and a quick remodel, it reopened. Advertisements on March 9, 1919, proudly proclaimed, "IDEAL THEATRE IS OPEN TODAY. It is Beautifully Decorated and Offers a Bright Welcome to All. FINE PLAYS are 'On Her Moment' and 'The Street of Seven Stars.' The opening of the Ideal Theater today at popular prewar admission prices will prove an innovation in the picture business of Cedar Rapids. Like in the past, there will be but one aim on the Owner's part and that is to please the Patrons. On this policy he is reopening the Ideal after nearly two years of closed doors. The public admission prices will be six cents to children and eleven cents to adults, this admission fee to include war tax."

By 1921, the theater had closed for good. Enterprise Box Company moved in, operating until the 1930s, when the building's owner opened Smid Hardware. Later, several other businesses operated on the premises,

The Ideal Theater. The signage today says the Ideal Social Hall and Joseph Mateju, Tailor. *Photo by Peter D. Looney.*

with Borgenson's Paint located there from the 1980s until the horrific flood of 2008.

After years of sitting vacant, in 2017, local businessman and entrepreneur Jon Jelinek cleaned out the building, remodeled it, and reopened it as the Ideal Social Hall.

COLONIAL THEATRE

All of the theaters in Cedar Rapids that had been built specifically to be theaters were on the east side of the river. That changed in 1914.

The Colonial Theatre was built at 106 Third Avenue SW, next door to the new Gatto Building. It was built with geometric brick and terra-cotta decorations to match the neighboring Gatto.

After twenty years of showing movies, the Colonial closed, and the solid building has been home to a succession of various businesses. The building still stands and most recently housed the Lederman Bail Bonds company.

The Colonial Theatre was built in 1914, and the building still stands as Lederman Bail Bonds. *Photo by Peter D. Looney.*

STRAND/STATE/WORLD PLAYHOUSE

With the success of the 1912 Palace Theater on Second Avenue, the owners, Ford and Diebold, built a new venue at 314 Third Avenue SE. Constructed of steel supporting beams and concrete, this structure was designed to last. And it has, for over one hundred years.

The Strand Theatre opened on October 18, 1915, with a seating capacity of 1,500, including the balcony and twelve opera boxes. Lavish murals from Greek mythology decorated the walls. It was the first theater in Cedar Rapids with a cantilevered single balcony, also constructed with steel beams. Earlier large theaters had been constructed with multiple shallow balconies with posts supporting them, resulting in partially blocked views.

The Strand was intended to be a legitimate performance theater with its own regular acting troupe, but soon, movies and vaudeville were the featured attractions. The Strand did well for fifteen years.

Empty yet solid and standing proudly is the building that housed the Strand, then the State and finally the World Playhouse. *Photo by Peter D. Looney.*

In 1930, the theater operations were sold to Paramount-Publix, and the theater was remodeled and renamed the State Theater. The opera boxes flanking the proscenium were removed during remodeling, and the curving exterior marquee was replaced. The theater went on to another long stretch of movie success.

In 1959, the theater again closed for modernizing and remodeling and reopened in 1960 with new management and a new name—the New World Playhouse, commonly referred to as the World. The screen was fitted for the much wider CinemaScope projection, and beautiful waterfalls were installed in the lobby.

After a twenty-one-year run showing Hollywood blockbuster movies, the World closed in 1981. It sat vacant for eighteen years, until 1999, when a church used the building for three years. Then the building owners began renovating the premises, with retail space being the goal. The slope was removed from the main floor, raising the level at the stage by five feet. A temporary drop ceiling was installed from the front edge of the balcony to the proscenium and then continuing above the stage area, effectively making it a one-story building.

In 2003, a teen nightclub and performance venue called the Nexus opened, where local bands (mostly high school and college kids) could perform. The intention was to also hold other types of performances and art exhibits, but nothing came to fruition. As of 2020, the building stands empty.

RKO IOWA/IOWA THEATRE CR

The Iowa Theater is a stately, four-story, reinforced concrete and steel structure built on the corner of First Avenue and Third Street SE and designed in neoclassical revival style for the Orpheum vaudeville chain. With its prominent thirty-foot ear of corn on the corner façade, lit with more than four thousand lights, the Iowa was an instant landmark. The 1,800-seat auditorium was uniquely wide, with all seats close to the stage, and the lobby was furnished with ornate antiques. The venue was also one of the first theaters with air conditioning.

The Iowa opened its doors on June 6, 1928, as a vaudeville and movie house. Live acts were performed in front of the silent movie screen to the accompaniment of a massive organ. The Rhinestone Barton Golden Voiced Bartola theater organ dominated the orchestra pit and is the only one of its type still in operation today. Cedar Rapids is one of the very few cities to have two working theater organs in its original installations. The other is the Mighty Wurlitzer in the Paramount Theatre.

In 1929, a year after it opened, vaudeville acts took a backseat to the more popular moving pictures with sound, as the Iowa became part of the RKO sound picture studio chain. RKO Radio Pictures was an American film production company formed just a year earlier by the three-way merger of the Keith-Albee-Orpheum (KAO) theater chain, the successful silent-era FBO Studios and Radio Corporation of America (RCA), which engineered the merger to create a market for the company's new sound on film technology.

For the next fifty years, the Iowa Theater was one of Cedar Rapids' largest and most popular movie houses. The RKO Iowa briefly attempted to revive vaudeville in the late '40s and occasionally hosted live shows. But attendance was falling off, and theaters all over were suffering from declining revenues.

In December 1965, the theater was leased to the Dubinsky Brothers, who undertook a quick remodel. More comfortable seats were brought in, as well as new paint and interior decorating. A larger screen was installed to improve the viewing of the new widescreen films. Now simply called the Iowa Theater, it reopened on Christmas Day 1965, with the James Bond movie *Thunderball*, starring Sean Connery.

Exterior modernizing of the building involved replacing the original "RKO Iowa" marquee over the sidewalk and removing the tall corn sign. The corn sign was put in storage but has since disappeared, probably for its scrap metal value.

The Iowa continued showing films for the next eighteen years but shut down on April 24, 1983. Shortly after closing its doors as a movie theater, the building became the new home for the Cedar Rapids Community Theatre. Over $2.5 million was raised in capital campaigns to adapt the facility to a 513-seat, handicap-accessible theater. Rehearsal space, dressing rooms, a new green room and administrative offices were added. Much of the original grandeur was retained while adding state-of-the-art lighting, sound and stage rigging systems.

In addition to the mainstage theater season, the facility stayed busy throughout the next twenty-five years with other events ranging from stand-up comedy to puppet shows to symphony chamber concerts. And then tragedy struck. In June 2008, the Iowa Theater was severely damaged by the worst flood in Cedar Rapids history. The theater quickly took center stage in the media, as it was often used as a visual on television and in newspapers to show the rise of water in downtown Cedar Rapids.

"The below-grade level of the Iowa Theater building was completely submerged by flood waters," explained Todd Dolphin, FEMA's Public Assistance branch chief. "This caused damage to interior walls and floor finishes, doors, electrical, and HVAC."

The waters eventually receded, and the recovery process began. Every effort was made to respect and save the history of the building. The ticket lobby had the 1965 decorations removed, and plaster work and lighting fixtures were restored to the 1928 appearance. New color schemes echoed earlier colors used by the theater. New rehearsal and dressing room spaces were added in the basement and upper levels of the building.

The elegant Iowa Theater building is now Theatre Cedar Rapids. *Photo by Peter D. Looney.*

The stage floor was rebuilt with a new removable trap section. New mechanicals were added and a new lift for the organ console was installed. The Barton was refurbished and proudly returned to the orchestra pit.

Original ornamental plaster details from 1928 that were hidden behind paneling were uncovered, restored and repainted. A new external marquee was installed with similar proportions to the original, which had been removed in the 1980s. The theater lobby was expanded into the storefronts of the building, resulting in a wider modern lobby that accommodates more patrons and displays photos from the theater's history.

The grand reopening of Theatre Cedar Rapids was held on February 26, 2010, with a production of *The Producers*. And the magic of live theater continues today.

CAPITOL/PARAMOUNT THEATRE

In 1928, this solid, redbrick, six-story building was built at 123 Third Avenue SE, and it remains an active theater today. The huge structure takes up more than a third of the block and includes sidewalk-level shops and plenty of upstairs office space, but its main feature is a magnificent auditorium that opened as the Capitol Theatre on September 1, 1928. With 1,900 seats and three floors of dressing rooms, this high-class venue was designed as a showcase for both stage acts and motion pictures.

The half-block-long lobby includes a hall of mirrors leading to a grand staircase, patterned after the Palace of Versailles in France. The lobby and lounge were filled with oil paintings from Europe, gilt mirrors, chests with marble and bronze busts, statues on pedestals, tables, sofas upholstered in blue and green velvet and gilded lamps. This was probably the closest most Cedar Rapidians would get to a palatial setting. The Capitol provided movies and live stage shows with a full range of vaudeville comedians, singers, dancers and acrobats, with musical accompaniment provided by either live musicians or the Mighty Wurlitzer organ.

A year after opening, the theater was sold to Paramount Studios and renamed the Paramount Theatre. By the 1930s, live acts were dropped. The huge screen and the roaring sound made it a perfect venue for Hollywood's top motion pictures. Matinees, uniformed ushers, newsreels and cartoons added to the experience.

By the 1960s, regular usage had taken its toll, and a multi-decade restoration project was begun to save the theater. Numerous improvements were made to the wall dressing, carpeting and lighting. The chandeliers, made of Austrian cut glass, were restored. In the auditorium, most of the seats were upholstered with red velvet. When completed in 1976, the theater was listed on the National Register of Historic Places. The showing of movies continued.

In 2003, the Paramount Theatre underwent an $8 million renovation. Updates included a wing space addition, a new HVAC system, new restrooms, plaster work repair, and electrical and fire system updates. The lobby, lounge area, concession space, restrooms and gathering spaces were improved to welcome patrons before shows and at intermission. The building continued to be a popular attraction.

Then the 2008 floodwaters came. At the crest of the flood, the building was inundated with approximately eight feet of water on the main level. The basement and subbasement were completely flooded, causing more than $16 million in damage to the historic building. After two years of cleaning and another two years of rebuilding, at a cost of $35 million, the Paramount Theatre reopened in the fall of 2012.

The restoration included updating the audience experience to modern standards, with wider seats, realigned aisles and accommodations for ADA compliancy. This crown jewel of Cedar Rapids is now a 1,700-seat multiuse theater, hosting concerts, fundraisers, dance recitals and Broadway shows. It is also home to Orchestra Iowa, the region's premier symphony orchestra.

TIMES THEATER

The 725-seat Times Theater at 1400 First Avenue SE opened on Christmas in 1941. This facility was not designed to be an elegant theater. It was a former parking garage that became a workhorse theater for the working class.

After nine years of operation, in 1950, Roy Metcalfe purchased the theater. Metcalfe was the president of a trade organization called the Allied Independent Theatre Owners of Iowa, Nebraska and South Dakota, and locally, he also operated the World Playhouse in Cedar Rapids.

With the advent of television in the 1950s, attendance at the theater started declining. It closed in 1964 for remodeling and reopened in 1965 as the New Times 70, with the first 70 mm projection equipment in the Cedar Rapids area. The seating capacity was reduced, allowing for staggered seats in rows that were forty inches apart, improving sight lines and increasing leg room.

The May 16, 1966 issue of the industry periodical *Boxoffice Magazine* published photos of the auditorium, lobby and lounge of the New Times 70 Theater. The auditorium, now with 523 seats, featured six abstract black light paintings on the side walls, satin drapes on the screen wall and a color scheme of emerald and aqua. The lobby was updated with walnut paneling, contemporary furniture and decorative panels of colored glass. The black and white floor tile extended into the restrooms.

A fascinating highlight in the life of the New Times 70 was its year-long run of *The Sound of Music*.

The movie theater operated until 1979, when it was sold and became an adult theater, the Times Triple XXX, showing projected videos. A decade later, it became a video rental store. The building was demolished in the early 1990s, and an Arby's fast food restaurant was built on the site in 1994.

PLAZA THEATER

After the Times opened in '41, twenty-six years passed before any new theaters were built in Cedar Rapids. Then, in 1967, a freestanding structure was built on the perimeter of Lindale Mall at 4444 First Avenue NE. The new Plaza Theater was "Incomparable in its Charm and Beauty!" This eight-hundred-seat, single-screen theater was one of three sturdy venues built in the 1960s by ABC/TriStates Theaters. The other two were in Moline and Des Moines.

The Plaza featured rocking chair seating, a large screen with drapes and 70 mm projection. According to former manager Mike Geater, "Because of their basic floor plan, they were extremely efficient to operate. I managed this theater for about a year, and relieved managers for vacations at the other two. I refer to these theaters, and others like them, as the 'second generation' of movie palaces."

Movie attendance fell off, and the theater closed in 1980. Quickly repurposed, the seats were removed, and the building became an office supply business for a short time. In 1990, it opened as a nightclub, Zazoo the Beach Club, but that only lasted a year. In 2002, it reopened as a ballroom called Let's Dance, which lasted four years before closing in 2006.

After standing empty, the flood of 2008 forced Theatre CR shows out of the flooded downtown Iowa Theater, and the Plaza building served as an excellent temporary location for CRCT for the next two years.

Following that, from 2012 to 2016, the building housed Planet X, offering laser tag, miniature golf, rock climbing and other family activities. Empty once again, the building awaits its next tenant.

JERRY LEWIS/EASTOWN CINEMAS I & II

In the late '60s, entertainer Jerry Lewis partnered with the Network Cinema Corporation to form a chain of theater franchises called Jerry Lewis Cinemas. The corporation would provide the know-how, name recognition and marketing, and franchisees would put up the money and the man-hours.

Lewis's theaters, branded "mini cinemas," followed a standardized model that called for one to three auditoriums with seating for around three hundred patrons each. While similar to the cracker box design of most '70s multiplexes, mini cinemas were generally a notch above their peers in decor and featured what could best be described as mid-level amenities—neither cheap nor luxurious.

By the mid-1970s, the chain had grown to two hundred sites, with another one hundred slotted for development. Despite the company's rapid growth, the overall venture was not having the expected success. Almost as quickly as the chain had spread throughout the country, the mini cinemas began to fold. Initially, owners cited the company's policy of only booking "family friendly" films as the problem, but the decline continued even after the policy was expanded to include more competitive booking practices.

Unfortunately, by 1980, the chain was completely defunct. (Thank you *Cinelog* for this informative history lesson.)

The Cedar Rapids location at 200 Collins Road NE, next to Kmart East, had opened in 1971 as the Jerry Lewis Cinema I & II. This was the first multiple-screen theater in town, and it's worth noting that every Cedar Rapids theater built since then has also had multiple screens. The Jerry Lewis only lasted about a year before new owners renamed it the Eastown I & II, which successfully showed movies and sold popcorn for twenty years, until the early '90s. But the ongoing problem of too many theaters, too little product and too much television led to its eventual demise.

The building was vacated, and it went on to have subsequent lives. The Play Station purchased it in 2008 and then remodeled and moved in. It remains there today as eastern Iowa's largest family fun center, popular for birthday parties, group outings and just plain fun.

STAGE 4 THEATERS

"See the Future Now in Cedar Rapids at the Stage 4! Unique and Intimate Atmosphere! Exquisite Decor, Parking Galore!" So heralded the arrival of the city's second multiple-screen theater in 1974. Situated clear across town from the Jerry Lewis Cinema, this multiplex was next door to Kmart west at 2945 Williams Parkway SW.

The Stage 4 Theater was opened by the Dubinsky Brothers. Sixteen years later, in 1990, it changed hands and was sold to Excellence Theatres. In 1995, operations were taken over by Carmike Cinemas, and the theater closed for good in 2000.

Capri Beauty & Barber College relocated from its downtown Cedar Rapids location into the building in 2001. The school remodeled it into a strikingly beautiful multi-level facility, and it remains there today.

ADULT THEATERS

During the '70s, the Cedar Rapids-Marion area was home to four adult theaters that offered X-rated films.

The Marion Garden Theater opened in 1914 and switched to adult fare only from 1972 to 1976, before returning to general movies. The West Post Cinema X opened in 1974 on the west edge of Cedar Rapids at 5415 Sixteenth Avenue SW and was renamed the Academy Adult Video in 1980. After closing, the location was home to a couple of bars before becoming a car dealership, which has remained for over twenty years. Danish Bookworld XXX was in operation at 1601 Sixth Street SW from 1977 to 1982. The building was originally a gas station, and after the adult cinema years, it was a used car dealership, followed by a tattoo shop. And as mentioned earlier, the Times Theater became an adult venue in 1979.

Now, back to family theaters.

WESTDALE I, II, III AND IV

The next multi-screen theater complex was the Westdale 4 at 2750 Edgewood Road SW on the south edge of the Westdale Mall property. The Westdale 4 opened in 1980 and was operated by General Cinemas. It was taken over by Excellence Theatres in the late '80s, and then in the early '90s, it was operated by Carmike Cinemas.

"This theater had four long, narrow auditoriums, with an aisle down the middle of each one. And they had uncomfortable white 'reclining' seats, and screens mounted way too high on the wall," according to the website Cinema Treasures.

The theater closed in 2000 and has housed a series of businesses and storefronts ever since.

LINDALE 6

The large neon sign on the front of the impressive new building next to the Hy-Vee grocery store behind Lindale Mall said, "Lindale Theatres." Opened by Excellence Theatres in 1989, it provided six screens to choose from.

The weeklong kick-off started Monday, December 18, showing free movies ("You've never had an offer this good!") starting at ten o'clock each morning with free coffee, donuts and cake. ("Moms—Bring the Kids! Kids—Bring Your Mom!")

The theater operated for twelve years before closing in 2001. It was remodeled and became the second location of Planet X, the arcade, rock climbing and laser tag venue, for the next decade. JoAnn Fabrics and Crafts took over the building in 2012 and remains there today.

CARMIKE 7

The Carmike 7 was the "Finest Theater in the Midwest," according to its advertisements. Owned and operated by the Carmike chain, it was built and opened in 1990 at 475 Northland Avenue NE. This theater featured "Bargain Matinees Daily—All Seats $2.50 before 5:30."

(A gentleman who shall remain unnamed had a daughter who worked here during her high school and college years. She may have occasionally brought home gigantic garbage bag–sized bags of leftover popcorn at the end of a long night. What a pleasant surprise for her parents to wake up to in the morning!)

After eighteen years, the Carmike 7 closed. Cedar Rapids' largest employer, Rockwell-Collins, took over the building in 2009, remodeling it into its employees' daycare center.

IMAX DOME THEATER

Iowa's first IMAX theater opened in March 2001 in Cedar Rapids under the name McLeod/Busse IMAX Dome Theatre. The Science Station had been created in 1986 in the old Central Fire Station at 427 First Street SE, and the 170-seat IMAX theater was added to the back of the building fifteen years later.

Offering science and nature movies on a six-story wraparound screen, IMAX technology was designed to fill more of your field of view than a conventional theater. With the crystal-clear Dolby sound and earth-shaking subwoofers, IMAX made movie watching an immersive experience.

The McLeod/Busse addition was designed by a new architectural firm, Olsen, Popa and Novak, now known as OPN Architects. The design was modernistic, with a façade of glazed glass walls enclosed by larger free-standing brick walls. IMAX theater construction differs significantly from

IMAX Dome Theater, today home to the Cedar Rapids Metro Economic Alliance. *Photo by Peter D. Looney.*

conventional theaters in that increased image resolution allows the audience seating to be much closer to the screen. The rows of seats are set at a steep angle so everyone in the audience is facing the screen directly.

According to a 2005 review on Judysbook.com, "The IMAX really does offer a unique movie-going experience. The shows are spectacular, and cover a wide variety of subjects. In addition, popular movies such as Batman can be seen here. The staff at the IMAX does a great job of moving people in and out quickly, and you can save some money if you purchase your IMAX ticket along with admission to the Science Station. It's a great way to spend an afternoon or evening!"

However, the costs of the construction and operation of the IMAX saddled the Science Station with debt it couldn't afford. When pledged support failed to come through and attendance lagged, the prospects were dim. In early 2008, the Science Station's board announced that it would close the McLeod/Busse IMAX Dome Theatre. "The staff made every effort to make the theater work, but ultimately we had to make this very difficult decision," said the president of the board.

Shortly after closing and the removal of the million-dollar electronic gear, the building was hit by the devastating 2008 flood. After a thorough cleanup and creative remodeling, the Cedar Rapids Chamber of Commerce took possession and moved in. It is now known as the Cedar Rapids Metro Economic Alliance.

DRIVE-IN THEATERS

"Hey kids—let's go to the drive-in!" C'mon, Mom and Dad, grab some snacks and beverages and maybe even pillows and the kids' jammies, pile into the car and head to the drive-in movie theater. "Oh boy—Fanta Orange!"

Or, if you're a teenager, cram a couple of buddies into the trunk, tell them, "Shhh," and be sure to look innocent when you pull in. Proud of the wheels you've been working so hard for? On evenings and weekends, be sure it's washed and waxed before you head to the drive-in.

Or if you're young lovers on a date, you'd better at least notice what movies are playing in case your parents ask you the next day.

Fresh air, the huge screen and the privacy of your own vehicle—and a trip or two to the snack bar. You're likely to run into your buddies there somewhere. And they always show multiple features at the drive-in—and maybe even a midnight show. Ah, those were the days.

Drive-in movie theaters brought some of the greatest advertising pitches: "Moonlight Lighting! No Parking Problems! Come as You Are! Bring the Whole Family! No Babysitter Problems—Bring 'em Along!"

There are only a couple of drive-in movie theaters remaining in Iowa today—none in Cedar Rapids. But back in the day, we had four to choose from.

Cedar Rapids Drive-In

The Drive-In Theater opened in 1949 and later became known as the Cedar Rapids Drive-In. It was located on the southwest edge of town at 2727 Sixteenth Avenue SW at the intersection of highways headed south and west out of town. The first drive-in in the area, it had an amazing capacity of six hundred cars. During the sixteen years of its existence, it introduced thousands of eastern Iowans to the fun and simplicity of drive-in movies.

Ads in the *Gazette* noted, "Movies in Living Color! A Miracle in Sound: In-Car Speakers, with Finger-Tip Volume Controls! Adult Admission: 60¢. Cars Free! Children Free! Plus 6 Bugs Bunny Cartoons!"

Tragically, the tornado that ripped through that part of town in 1965 completely destroyed the screen, and it was never rebuilt. After the area was cleared, Kmart west was built there, which eventually closed and became home to Mid-American Aerospace in 2018.

This aerial photo focuses on Lindale Mall and shows the location of the Twixt Town Drive-In directly to the north. *Courtesy of the History Center, Linn County Historical Society.*

Twixt Town Drive-In

The Twixt Town Drive-In Theater was in operation from 1952 to 1976, located at 1400 Twixt Town Road NE, which is now Collins Road Square shopping center. If you've ever wondered where the name Twixt Town came from, it happened to be the road splitting Cedar Rapids from Marion—between, betwixt or just twixt the two towns.

Advertisements for the theater teased that there would be "Two Shows Nightly, with a Special Midnight Show Every Saturday! The Midnight Show is at No Extra Charge!"

The 1965 tornado that wiped out the Cedar Rapids Drive-In across town also damaged the Twixt Town. But a new, $20,000 screen was erected, and the Twixt Town was back in the business of showing movies for another eleven years.

Collins Road Drive-In

The Collins Road Drive-In Theater was an extremely popular spot from 1967 to 1986. It was behind Hall Home Furnishings at 1566 Collins Road NE and is now the location of the McGrath car dealership headquarters and car lot. Ads from the day the drive-in opened claimed it was "Iowa's Finest Outdoor Theater" and had "the Largest Movie Screen in Iowa!"

Cedar Rapids Twin Drive-In Theaters

Once you decided which movie you preferred to see, you could double your pleasure if you parked near the rear of either the Twin East or the Twin West Drive-In Theaters. You could watch two movies at once as long as you didn't mind swiveling your head to watch the movie behind you and being unable to hear it. Speaking from this author's personal experience, you would sometimes come to the conclusion that the movie behind you was better than the movie in front of you. So, you'd hang up your speaker, start up your car, drive out of the exit, drive in the entrance to the other theater, pay again, find a new place to park and settle down to watch the movie. Of course, most of the movies were grade B movies, so they were all generally lousy. But an evening at the drive-in was less about art and more about the adventure. Ah, the carefree days of youth and disposable income.

The opening night newspaper ads stated, "An Entertainment Star is Born—the Ultimate in Drive-in Theaters—Two Big Screens to Choose From—High-Fidelity Sound—Automated Projectors—Modern Snack Bar."

Situated on Highway 218 South at 6300 Sixth Street SW, the Twin was in operation from 1969 to 1987. It has since been torn down and is now the site of an industrial park.

TODAY'S THEATERS

Today, people are inclined to stay home and watch movies in the comfort of their own homes on their big digital flat screens or on their laptops or other electronic devices. Maybe they'll run to the corner and rent the latest DVD release from Redbox. Or they'll find something on cable or satellite. Maybe they'll browse the selection on Netflix.

But if you want an evening out, because as we're all aware, there's no better popcorn than movie theater popcorn, you'll be happy to know there are still three movie theaters in town as of May 2020.

Visit the Collins Road 5 Theaters, which opened in 1987. Located at 1462 Twixt Town Road NE in Collins Road Square, this five-screen theater was built on the site of the old Twixt Town Drive-In. Enjoy affordable second-run movies. It sometimes shows "Free Kids Movies All Summer Long" and "$4 Tuesdays, Plus Popcorn for Only $1!"

Or visit the AMC Classic Westdale 12 Theater at 2435 Edgewood Road SW by Westdale Mall. This spot was originally named the Wynnsong 12 when its twelve screens opened in 1999. You will enjoy "WIDE-Screen Entertainment, All Auditoriums in DIGITAL Sound, with Plush High-Back Chairs, and Wide Aisle Seating featuring Cupholders," as well as "Computerized Advance Ticket Sales."

Or check out Marcus Cinema at 5340 Council Street NE, the city's newest movie venue with sixteen wall-to-wall curved screens, explosive digital sound and "Films, Family and Fun like Never Before!" It was built as the Galaxy 16 in 2004 and changed owners in 2018.

Folks, that's thirty-three screens to choose from right here in Cedar Rapids, Iowa!

2

DANCE HALLS AND BALLROOMS

Dick Clark's 'American Bandstand' spread the gospel of American pop music and teenage style that transcended the regional boundaries of our country and united a youth culture that eventually spread its message throughout the entire world.
—John Oates

Music is the soundtrack of your life.
—Dick Clark

An' a one, an' a two…
—Lawrence Welk

Almost everyone loves listening to music, and most music lovers enjoy hearing music performed live. Theaters, civic auditoriums, colleges, schools, churches, fraternal organizations, clubs and taverns have all offered various forms of live music. And when the music is good and has a beat, some folks are compelled to leap to their feet and dance.

Dancing has always been part of American culture. Every city across the country seemed to have at least one ballroom or dance hall featuring live musicians playing a range of music, from classical orchestral music to strict tempo ballroom dance music to big band to jazz to western swing to fiddle and accordion country to, eventually, rock-and-roll.

Music lovers found their entertainment at dance halls. Defining what was or was not a dance hall is a matter of personal preference. To some, a dance hall was any building where dances were held, even if it might be billed as a ballroom. For others, it was not a ballroom unless it had a certain ambiance.

Regardless, many of them became cultural landmarks. You're someplace special, the music is respected and honored and you're dancing. It's an encompassing experience.

Saturday nights were dance nights in most towns. Some ballrooms held dances two or three times a week, some more often, depending on demand. As the dance popularity grew, so did the number of places to dance. Lots of bars and clubs offered live music and dancing, but the main purpose of those places was alcohol sales. Some of the larger hotels had ballrooms, for instance, the Crystal Ballroom at the Montrose, the Silver Leaf at the Magnus and the Roosevelt Ballroom.

By the late '70s and early '80s, the ballrooms and rock-and-roll dance halls were fading away, and discos were all the rage. In Cedar Rapids, that was Oscar's, Bugsy's and Gatsby's. Today, there are still plenty of places to hear good music and get up and dance, but we'll look at the lost ballrooms and dance halls.

ALAMO BALLROOM

Alamo Park was Cedar Rapids' first amusement park, built on the west side of town in 1906 on Thirteenth Street NW between B and E Avenues, where Roosevelt Middle School now sits. It was dubbed "a superb place of legitimate recreation for respectable people."

The dance pavilion was promoted as the largest in Iowa and was instantly popular. But a few years later, with the addition of gambling and alcoholic beverages available in the park, it became a less-than-desirable place to hang out. The dance pavilion and the entire Alamo Park closed in 1913 after only seven years of operation.

For the next thirteen years, from 1913 to 1926, there were no floors in Cedar Rapids that were dedicated to dancing. Oh, there were plenty of bars, taverns, social clubs and auditoriums where dances were held and dancing was available, but there were no venues devoted to the important pastime of dancing. And then Danceland and Linger Longer arrived on the scene.

DANCELAND

The Majestic Storage building was a huge two-story brick and steel structure on the corner of A Avenue and Third Street NE. Built in 1912, it housed a series of offices, storage spaces, auto garages, car painting and other automobile-related businesses. It was next door to New Process Laundry, which later became Cedar Rapids Surplus Shop. In the early years, the Majestic Theater was right across the street. Years later, a popular bowling alley occupied the ground floor of the Majestic Storage building.

In 1926, the building's entire second floor was opened, cleaned, remodeled and named Danceland. It quickly became *the* place for music and dancing. The owners had success with other ballrooms across the country, including Dreamland and Manhattan Beach in New York City, and were determined to create a high-class dance hall, a showcase for good music and a destination for midwestern music lovers.

The original decor had a Spanish theme in the main lounge, including striped awnings, wrought-iron sconces and railings, comfortable seating and a red floor. The large ballroom was a massive expanse of maple flooring with a stage at one end and chairs and tables surrounding the floor. It could accommodate many as eight hundred couples.

All of the important national acts of the day flocked to play here. In the early days, great orchestras were brought in to provide the music. In the '50s and '60s, the rock-and-rollers and pop acts became the headliners, with the best local bands and musicians performing as well.

Their buses, vans and trailers would unload into the back of the building from the elevated ramp on the A Avenue viaduct. Patrons would enter from the Third Street main entrance through the red double doors under the steel and neon marquee and then climb the wide set of stairs to the dance hall. At the top of the stairs, patrons were greeted by a colorful poster advertising the next concert. These unique cardboard concert posters were hand painted and often included an original photo of the artist.

Some of the big names that performed at Danceland over the years include Count Basie, Louie Armstrong, Glenn Miller, Duke Ellington, Johnny Cash, Wanda Jackson, Porter Wagoner, Conway Twitty, Eddie Cochran, the Everly Brothers, Chuck Berry, Buddy Holly, Roy Orbison, Bobby Darin, Frankie Avalon, the Four Seasons, the Animals, the Turtles, Jay and the Americans and Bobby Sherman.

Area musicians also provided dance music, including local favorites, such as Kenny Hofer, the Escorts, Al's Untouchables, the Legends, the Stompers, the Showmen and the Orphans.

In the late '30s, the hall was extensively remodeled with the bright colors and Art Deco styles that were popular at the time. The building was again remodeled in the '50s and updated to mid-century pop decor. Several years later, the building's exterior was covered with white aluminum panels.

During the late '50s, a television program modeled on Dick Clark's *American Bandstand* was shot there on Sunday afternoons. Shown on KCRG channel 9, local television and radio personality Jim Young, who had stood in for Dick Clark on *American Bandstand* at least once while he was on vacation, was the host. Bands played, teenagers danced and if you couldn't go, you could watch it from home.

In 1959, the national touring Winter Dance Party featuring Buddy Holly, Ritchie Valens and the Big Bopper were scheduled at Danceland for February 6. After their tragic plane crash on February 2, Dion & the Belmonts and Frankie Avalon replaced them for the Cedar Rapids show.

Danceland's final event was held in March 1968, and then the ballroom closed for good. The room stood empty for two years while the bowling alley remained open downstairs, but the building was demolished in 1973.

LINGER LONGER/MAY VU/RED BARN/ELLIS BALLROOM

First, go back in time fifty years and then go to Ellis Park. Go the west side of the park—to Ellis Golf Course. Zika Avenue cuts through the center of the course. Go west on Zika for about a mile, turn to the right and pull into 2500 Zika Avenue NW. You are now at the site of a dance pavilion that served Cedar Rapids dancers for forty years.

In 1927, Ernest and Beulah Henecke built a nice enclosed pavilion for dancing next to their house on their three and a half acres. They named it Linger Longer. It wasn't heated, so it was only used from July to September. Dances were held every Friday evening at the pavilion, and it was used for private parties, wedding dances, receptions, lodge outings, company picnics, fundraisers and, later on, teenage sock hops.

After seventeen years, in 1944, the Heneckes sold the property. The new owners renamed it MayVu Ballroom and continued the traditions. The music flowed, people danced, and parties were enjoyed.

Eighteen years later, new owners Nellie Sheftic Bennett and Jean Carney renamed it the Red Barn Ballroom and reopened it for business in the spring of 1963. The dancers kept dancing.

In the summer of 1966, the venue had new owners and another new name, Ellis Ballroom, and the focus was on teen dances. But by the next summer, Nellie Bennett was once again operating and promoting the Red Barn Ballroom, still offering teen dances.

Late in '67, there was another new owner, a Mr. Youngman. Unable to make a profit, the old building became the Red Barn Auction House before burning to the ground in 1968.

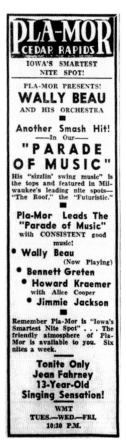

PLA-MOR BALLROOM

The next dance hall to open in Cedar Rapids was called the Pla-Mor. Built in 1889, the old auditorium, situated along the river at 127 First Street NE, offered roller-skating from 1909 to 1934. Then the rink closed, and in 1935, the Pla-Mor Ballroom opened. It was a great spot for a ballroom with the downtown location, the majestic structure and the in-house kitchen facilities.

The Pla-Mor was promoted as "Iowa's Smartest Nightspot," "Where Discriminating People Meet Their Friends," "Dancing every night except Monday," "Superb Theatrical Floor Show" and "Kitchen, featuring popular Italian and American dishes."

Events included charity balls, carnival nights, a flood relief dance for the American Red Cross for flood-devastated East Coast states (it raised $43.10), wedding anniversary parties, parish parties, political club events and beauty contests.

It stated that "Pabst Blue Ribbon Beer, White Soda, and Ginger Ale are exclusively served at the Pla-Mor."

Above: The Auditorium was home to the Auditorium Skating Rink from 1909 to 1934 and later the Pla-Mor Ballroom and even later the Eagles Club. *Courtesy of the History Center, Linn County Historical Society.*

Opposite: A Cedar Rapids *Gazette* ad from February 28, 1937, features a Parade of Music event offered at Pla-Mor. *Courtesy of the* Gazette.

In 1939, the Pla-Mor switched back to roller-skating during the spring and summer, only to return to dancing for the winter of 1939–40 under new management. But Pla-Mor closed for good in the summer of 1940. That same year, the auditorium's grand entrance dome was removed. The building's interior was also remodeled and became home to a variety of groups—the Civil Air Patrol; School Safety Patrol; Eagles Club; and various other parties, dances, meetings and exhibitions—for another thirty years. In 1969, it was demolished.

CEDAR PARK BALLROOM

Just south of the Marion city limits, on Marion Boulevard, was a large outdoor facility called Cedar Park. This location was later the site of Ce-

Cedar Park Ballroom ad from the *Cedar Rapids Gazette. Courtesy of the* Gazette.

Mar Acres and, much later, Jack's and Shopko. Today, it is home to the M.A.C. fitness club.

Starting in 1921 as an open space for midway shows, the first Cedar Park "building" was simply a large tent that was erected for dances and other events requiring shelter from the elements. Eventually, a hardwood floor was installed under the tent, and in 1932 the facility became the Wigwam Roller Rink. Soon, a permanent roof went up, and the open-sided auditorium hosted additional events such as boxing and wrestling. Then the sides were enclosed, including large windows that would swing open.

In 1936, the building was enlarged and reopened as Cedar Park Ballroom and was promoted as the Plaza of Amusement. The Plaza included an adjacent two thousand-seat open-air arena that presented traveling vaudeville revues, with boxing and wrestling as weekly features on Fridays.

National and regional orchestras and bands supplied the music for the dancers at Cedar Park, which was open for dancing every night from nine o'clock until one o'clock. An outdoor parlor called Tavern on the Green offered old-style lager beer, Sun-Shine Brand pop and "tasty food cooked on a butane gas stove," which was provided by Spryncl's. Completing the outdoor plaza were a few amusement rides and the nearby Cedar Grove picnic area.

When the ballroom first opened, admission was "Gents 40 cents, Ladies 15 cents." A year later, it was operating under new management, and admission had skyrocketed to "Men 75 cents, Ladies 40 cents." But the patrons continued to come.

Cedar Park Ballroom offered music, dancing and entertainment for four years. The building was then converted back to a skating rink, called Cedar Park Rink, which later became the Ce-Mar Roller Rink.

THORNWOOD BALLROOM

The fraternal society the Benevolent and Protective Order of Elks (BPOE, commonly known as the Elks Lodge) has always been an outstanding charitable and service organization. The downtown Cedar Rapids Lodge also had a summer lodge located at 1222 Hawthorne Drive SW, which was just southeast of Czech Village.

The summer lodge, built in 1930, also went by the name Thornwood and began offering live music and dancing. In the mid-'30s, the lodge was promoted as the Riverview Park Pavillion, eventually reverting to the better-known name of Thornwood Ballroom. By 1938, it had become a prominent area dance hall. Orchestras and big bands performed there regularly, and dancing was offered six nights a week. National acts and popular radio bands put the Thornwood on their regular touring schedule.

By the '60s, the interest in big band music had begun to wane. But the story actually gets better. The facility was ready for a new life, and in 1963, it became Art & Bob's Home Run Club.

Art "Superman" Pennington was a local Cedar Rapids baseball legend who played for Negro League teams in the 1940s. He played with the likes of Jackie Robinson, Satchel Paige, Hank Aaron and Willie Mays. He was a three-time league all-star. Pennington then played in the American Minor League and on several international teams before retiring from professional baseball in 1959. Art Pennington returned to Cedar Rapids, and in 1963, he opened his Home Run Club, which was the city's first fully integrated restaurant, music and dance venue.

Pennington was a popular figure in town and was honored numerous times at Cedar Rapids baseball games and city events. "Like so many other famous and little known legends, Mr. Pennington paved the way to brighter tomorrows," his website reads. "He truly is a civil rights legend and an American giant."

"The one thing that always stuck with me about Art was wondering what would have happened with him, baseball-wise, if it had been 40 years later," said longtime Kernels general manager Jack Roeder. "And he always had such charisma. He walked into a room, and he took command."

Mr. Pennington later operated Art's Home Run Cafe at 1200 Fifth Street SE.

TOP HAT

The Top Hat diner and night club was active from 1938 to 1945. It was located in the Coffits Building at 419 Second Avenue SE. The Top Hat promoted and advertised dancing and orchestra music.

Coffits was built in 1903 as an ice cream and confections factory. The building had many lives, including car sales, piano sales, and a cafeteria. Prior to the Top Hat, it had been home to the Hi Ho Tavern night club. After its time as Top Hat, it became a game and recreation facility and then a Sherwin Williams paint store. Since 1976, it has been home to Hall Bicycles.

The Top Hat Diner & Night Club was in the Coffits Building, now Hall Bicycle. *Photo by Peter D. Looney.*

KINGSTON BALLROOM

Other than the Thornwood, not many dance clubs were located on the west side of the river. But one building converted its upstairs hall into a ballroom.

The King Building at 213 First Street SW, which backed up to the river, had housed many businesses during its existence. The West Side Theatre was there in 1914, Norris & Kerr Auto Supplies operated there in the early '20s, the Cedar Rapids Police was headquartered there during the late '20s and the first floor was converted into a tavern in the 1940s. McSwiggan Tastryt Restaurant & Tavern (you have to say that "Tastryt" word out loud to really appreciate its cleverness) was replaced by Lipp's Tastryt Tavern by 1942. This became known as Lipp's Grill during the 1950s. It was more popularly known as one of the locations of the Local 100 Club in the '60s, before that whole strip of buildings along the river was torn down in 1969.

The second floor of the King Building was an open auditorium, and in the early 1900s, that upstairs space carried the west side–appropriate moniker of Kingston Hall, with the address 213½ First Street SW. By 1940, the second floor was the site of a popular dance hall called the Kingston Ballroom, later turning into the Ruptured Duck Club in the '50s.

ARMAR BALLROOM

Along with Danceland downtown, Armar Ballroom was the other long-lasting, hugely successful dance hall in Cedar Rapids.

Armar Ballroom was built in 1948 by an experienced ballroom owner from Des Moines, Tom Archer. He used the first two letters of his last name and the first three letters of the town of Marion to create the name "Armar." It was located on the border between Marion and Cedar Rapids on First Avenue, where Applegate's Landing was later built and Carlos O'Kelly's sits today—behind Cibo Fusion (formerly Denny's) and Ohnward Bank & Trust (formerly United Security Savings Bank). It was built right next to Ce-Mar Acres, which had just converted the old Cedar Park Ballroom into a roller-skating rink.

With its big, arched roof, the building had the look and shape of an airplane hangar and included an upstairs apartment for the ballroom's manager. With seating for 1,500 and a house capacity of 3,000, this house could get rockin'. It had a dance floor made of maple, and tiered booths so the seated patrons could always see the band and watch the dancers.

Armar was part of the national big band circuit for almost thirty years, bringing in the country's biggest names while also offering rock & roll and country music. The biggest night of the year was always New Year's Eve, when the patron count might exceed the posted capacity by another five hundred people or so.

Other events regularly held there were wedding dances, banquets, luncheons, conventions, variety shows and fashion shows. Armar was also a regular venue for political events and fundraisers. In early 1965, it became a roller-skating rink for a few months before returning to its focus on music.

Armar closed after the final New Year's Eve show on December 31, 1976. In two years, the building was gone, streets were platted and poured and various new businesses had been built.

MELODY INN DANCE HALL

The Melody Inn was situated in an old two-story frame building behind the ZCBJ building in NewBo, at 329 Twelfth Avenue SE. For one hundred years—throughout the entire 1900s—the building was a tavern and dance hall, and its patrons were the hardworking blue-collar workers in the area. Across the street to the north was a foundry, across the street to the east was a steel factory and two blocks to the south was a packing house.

Over the years, the name of the club changed many times, often reverting to the Melody Inn moniker. The focus may not have always been on dancing, but it was enough to earn the designation of a dance hall. The following is a partial list of businesses that operated the venue, starting with the brothers who opened the first tavern in 1900:

Sindelar Tavern, Joseph and Ignatz Sindelar (1900)
Bervad's Tavern, Adolph Bervad (1927)
Down Town Village (1933–34)
Twelfth Avenue Beer Parlor (1936)
Snyder's Dine & Dance (1940–46)
Melody Inn & Dance Hall (1950–56)
Charlie's (1956–57)
Melody Inn Tavern (1958–59)
Rag Time Inn (1960)
Melody Inn (1962–69)
Marty's Ballroom & Tap (1969)
Red Carpet Lounge (1971)
Russo's Melody Inn (1972–75)
Talk of the Town (1976–77)
Watering Hole (1981–84)
JR's Place (1985–91)
Attitude Lounge (1993–98)

By 1998, the old building was rundown and empty, and the property was needed for parking. The popular Third Street Live rock club was beginning its ten-year run, and the Chrome Horse Slophouse & Saloon was under development—both located in the ZCBJ building. The old Melody Inn building was demolished.

Ten years later, in 2018, a new four-story mixed-use structure called the 329 Building, housing retail, office and condos, was built on the exact spot of the Melody Inn.

ARROWHEAD BALLROOM

Back in the day, before it was a major northern Cedar Rapids artery, Blairs Ferry Road was a gravel road that headed west out of south Marion toward Hiawatha, the Cedar River and, eventually, Palo. Mr. Blairs's ferry had sunk in the Cedar long ago. Anyway, in 1964, as businesses along the road started developing, an indoor archery facility called Arrowhead Archery Lanes opened at 260 Blairs Ferry Road.

After three years, the owners expanded their operations and usage of the building. Arrowhead Ballroom opened in 1967 as a public dance hall, offering live music and dancing on weekends with a focus on teens. Though it was only open for two years, folks today still remember the good times they had there dancing, rock and rolling and listening to local and top national bands.

City Furniture took over the building in 1970, and today, Stuff Etc. is situated near that location.

ZAZOO THE BEACH CLUB/LET'S DANCE

As noted in chapter 1, the Plaza Theater was built in 1967 by Lindale Mall, next door to the Firestone tire store. In 1980, the building's usage began changing, first becoming a short-lived office supplies store.

In 1990, after extensive remodeling, it opened as a night club called Zazoo the Beach Club, with a huge dance floor, but that lasted barely a year.

A decade later, in 2002, it reopened as a legitimate dance hall named Let's Dance, offering a "Smoke-Free Dance Hall, and a Huge Free-Floating

Hardwood Dance Floor." Regularly featured dance events included palace ballroom, rock spot, top 40 club night, ladies' country night, hip-hop and R&B, DJ dance party and karaoke. Live bands provided some of the music.

Let's Dance closed four years later in 2006. From 2008 to 2010, Theatre CR used the facility as its temporary home, after the 2008 flood. Next, the building was Planet X from 2013 to 2016, offering laser tag, miniature golf and other family activities. Today the building is empty, awaiting its next tenant.

THE COUNTRY CLUB

A couple of buildings went up side by side on Sixth Street in 1973. The first one, at 3203 Sixth Street SW, was Lancer Lanes, and is still open for bowling forty-five years later.

The building that went up next door was a roller rink called Skate Country at 3233 Sixth Street SW. After twenty-four years, in 1994, the roller rink closed.

But the Skate Country building had more entertainment to provide to Cedar Rapidians and reopened in 1995 as the Country Club Night Club. Advertisements made sure locals were aware that it was all about country dancing—and it was, in fact, "Two Steps Above the Rest." So, pull on your cowboy hat and boots and your Levi's, grab your partner and let's two-step around the room. The Club was also a great place to learn country line dancing.

It closed in 1999 and became Leisure Time Billiards & Sports Bar before the building was eventually torn down. The lot is empty today.

ELEMENT DANCE CLUB

Something new to Iowa was experimented with in 1956. It was called a "shopping center." Until then, stores would be clustered in downtown areas, plus there would be small grocery stores and shops scattered throughout residential neighborhoods. But in 1956, just north of the city limits in the farmland between Cedar Rapids and Marion, along the Marion Boulevard, the Town & Country Shopping Center was built. There were thirty stores congregated in this long L-shaped structure anchored by May's Drug on the south and Sun Mart on the north. The experiment was a success, and now, shopping centers, malls and plazas are everywhere.

Built into this shopping center, right next to Sun Mart, was a fairly large retail space, and over the years, various businesses were situated there, including Morris Plan Loans, Mercy Fitness Center and a rock music venue. But in 2005, it became a dance club.

The owners of Third on First, located in the old Sambo's building in the parking lot, also owned Third Base Sports Bar on Blairs Ferry. When two spaces sharing an entrance opened in Town & Country, they grabbed them. The smaller space was a long, narrow bar called the Blarney Stone, later called the Hub. The larger space next to it became the Element Dance Club.

Operating from 2005 to 2009, this was the hot spot for dancing. Have you ever been in a modern discotheque? I'll let the online magazine *Thump* describe what the dance club experience was like:

> *You know the feeling: you're in the club, the music coursing through your veins like liquid anticipation. Dry ice, plumes of cigarette smoke, and flecks of Old Spice are mingling in the air and curling up your nostrils. You want to move, to dance across the floor, manifesting the pounding music in physical form, only your muscles are tense, your brow furrowed, and instead you stand watching everybody else, one clammy hand clinging to a plastic cup. Dancing in a nightclub is all about showing off your body, and if you don't dress to impress, that just ain't gonna happen. Say it once more so I know you've understood…you dressed to impress. And then you DANCE. It's your mom in a gospel choir, it's a school musical, it's a Cliff Richard arena tour…it's the step clap. A simple, elegant move, guaranteed to say "Hey, I might look too old to be here, but I can move like a four year old!" Ah! And there it is! The fruits of your labors and the culmination of any good night of dancing in the club: a big old fashioned grind chain, snaking off into the distance as far as the eye can see. Oh, what a night! What a time to be alive!*

But time moves on and things change. The club closed, and the rock venue First Avenue Live took over for a couple of years. Then that section of the building was torn down, and in 2015, a new Fareway grocery store was built in its spot.

So, if you find yourself wanting to groove and shake your booty as you're pushing a shopping cart down the aisles of this Fareway, now you know why.

OTHER DANCE HALLS

Over the years, there were quite a few other ballrooms in nearby eastern Iowa towns—some a short drive and others a legitimate road trip but worth the drive if you wanted to enjoy even more live music and dancing. You've probably heard of, and maybe even been to, some of these:

Dance-Mor: Originally opened for business as the Paramount Dance Pavilion (Swisher)
Library Ballroom: Next door to the Ranch Supper Club (Cou Falls)
Prairiemoon Ballroom: Originally a roller-skating rink (Prairieburg)
Ponderosa Ballroom: Originally Hofer's Ballroom (Walford)
Hi-Way Gardens (Stanwood)
Langs Barn Dance (Lisbon)
Green Barn (Shueyville)
Electric Barn (Anamosa)
Hawk Ballroom (Coralville)
Loops Ballroom (Monticello)
Mardon Ballroom (Hopkington)
Gayla Ballroom (Independence)
Dance Royale Ballroom (Fairfax)
Wapsi Moon Dance Pavilion (Waubeek)
Empire Ballroom (Manchester)
Sherman Ballroom (Norway)
Hiland Palace (Columbus Junction)

And don't forget the youth and teen clubs in Cedar Rapids, which were at the peak of their popularity in the '60s and '70s. Kids want to dance too, so several places were focused on youth, music, dancing, fun, games and activities, adult supervision and no alcohol. They usually had an organization sponsoring them, and they all tended to have short life spans. The following is a partial list:

Attic Teen Club: 119 ½ Third Avenue SE, upstairs—next to the Paramount (1969)
Church/Teen Dances: Pioneer and Thirtieth Street SE, near Monroe School (early 1970s)
Club NRG: Way out at 5101 Sixteenth Avenue SW (2002)
Gizmo's: 3901 First Avenue SE, in the Gin Mill building (1984)

Guys 'n Gals Teen-Age Club: Sixteenth Avenue SW, by the drive-in (1960)

Keen Teen Club: In the YMCA, First Avenue and Fifth Street NE (1960s)

Sailin' Shoes: 3223 Sixteenth Avenue SW (1979)

Teen Canteen: Eleventh Street in Marion by Ole's Ham & Egger (1960s)

Teen Club/Riverside Park Rec Center: First Street SW (1960)

Teen Club: In the CSPS Hall, Third Street SE (1968–72)

Teen Club: 1335 Ninth Street NW, near Ellis A&W (1971–73)

TJ's Teen Club: 711 Second Avenue SE, upstairs above Rapids Reproductions (1970s)

Y Teen's Club: YWCA (1950s)

3

BOWLING ALLEYS

There's kind of a Zen aspect to bowling. The pins are either staying up or down before you even throw your arm back. It's kind of a mind-set. You want to be in this perfect mind-set before you release the ball.
—Jeff Bridges

Bowling is a game for everyone. It's inexpensive and entertaining, and you can go bowling with a group, friends or family or by yourself. One of the parts is that you can play it without having to learn many rules. Roll the ball, don't step over the line and knock down the pins. A strike is when all the pins are knocked down on the first roll, and a spare is when any remaining pins are knocked over on the second roll. The maximum score is three hundred, which is achieved by getting twelve strikes in a row. The game is so simple yet so sophisticated that bowling is often referred to as an art. What a great pastime.

Plus, bowling alleys are open year-round.

The following is a list of the multitude of bowling alleys in the Cedar Rapids area over the years, followed by a more thorough discussion of Tropic Lanes, which shared the Danceland building for over thirty years.

Bowling: Downtown at 120 First Avenue NE (around 1900)
Cedar Rapids Bowl: Town & Country, First Avenue SE, basement level.
   The sidewalk entrance looked like you were going down to a subway (1956–75). Town & Country Bowl (1976–97)

Cedar Rapids Bowling Center: 265 Blairs Ferry Road NE, also offers outdoor volleyball (1978–present)

Eclipse Bowling: In the Jim Block building on Third Street NE, across from Danceland (1902–04)

Hach Bowling Alley: In the Hach Tavern building, corner of Second Street SE and Fourteenth Avenue (1924–33)

Jim Block Bowling: Also in the Jim Block building (1916–26)

Jubilee Lanes: Twixt Town Road (1958–2000)

Lancer Lanes: 3203 Sixth Street SW (1973–present)

Legion Lanes: Downtown on Fourth Avenue SE, south of Greene Square Park (1955–92)

Lincoln Bowling: Upstairs above the Tycoon, Duck Pin style (1924–64)

Marion Bowl: Marion Shopping Center (1961–74), Castle Lanes (1974–2013)

Marion Duck Pin Bowl: In the basement of the Central Market/Maid-Rite (1940s)

May City Lanes: Sixteenth Avenue SW and Williams Boulevard (1960–80), Empire Lanes (1981–86), May City Bowling Center (1987–present)

Parlor City Recreation Bowling: Downstairs below the Tycoon (1945–59)

Subway Bowling Alleys: Third Avenue SE, which was later the Flame Room (1921–43)

Westdale Bowling: 2020 Scotty Drive SW (1984–2019)

RED CROWN/BOWLIUM/TROPIC LANES

Ten years after Danceland took over the top floor of the Majestic Storage building at 124 Third Street NE, a bowling alley opened on the ground floor. Taking over the spaces formerly occupied by automotive-related service garages and storage facilities, Red Crown Bowling opened for business in 1937, with Brunswick alleys and human pinsetters. It offered the Red Crown Lounge as a cozy place to take a break and grab a beverage. A year later, the Coney Island Grill also opened.

By 1946, the alley had a new name, Bowlium, and the lounge was renamed the Gold Room. The Coney Island became the Bowlium Grill. A twenty-foot vertical sign was hung on the northwest corner of the building, suggesting, "Try Bowling for Health!"

New owners took over in 1953 and completely remodeled and updated the facility. Now called Tropic Lanes Bowling, the lounge and the grill became the Tropics and lasted until 1963, when it became the Polynesian-style Islander Bar. Bowling, fun, beverages and relaxation continued for another seven years.

As the City of Cedar Rapids was preparing for urban renewal in 1968, it purchased the building. Danceland closed, while Tropic Lanes remained open for two more years. Finally, the building was demolished in 1973. By then, most of the block, including Cedar Rapids Surplus, the old Grand Hotel, the Town Theater and the Norva Hotel had all been torn down, and by 1979, the Five Seasons Center—now the US Cellular Center—stood in its place.

4
ROLLER-SKATING RINKS

All skate!
—Every roller rink everywhere.

In case you didn't know, roller-skating is "the traveling on surfaces with roller skates." Now you know. You're welcome. It's a recreational activity as well as an international sport and can also be a form of transportation.

The first public roller-skating rinks were opened in the United States in the 1860s. Rink floors were made of wood or smooth concrete and, later, heavy-duty polyurethane plastic coating. By the 1930s, skating had become an extremely popular pastime. Its popularity lasted well into the 1960s. Then, in the 1970s, disco music–oriented roller rinks were all the rage across the country.

It's fun family entertainment for all ages. Always remember to skate in the same direction as the other skaters. This will help avoid head-on collisions and ensure the safety of all skaters. Again, you're welcome.

LYON FIFTH AVENUE RINK

When roller-skating rinks began spreading across the United States, one opened on Fifth Avenue SE in Cedar Rapids in 1884. The rink is mentioned in the city directory and in the newspapers because, even though it was advertised as "open to all," in 1885, it refused to admit a gentleman because he was black, claiming that a private business could refuse anyone it pleased. A lawsuit made it to Iowa's supreme court, which sided with the rink—a sad but common occurrence of the times. That type of bad decision was eventually corrected by civil rights laws.

CENTRAL SKATING RINK

This rink is also mentioned in the 1884 Cedar Rapids directory and was associated with a gymnasium. The directory names two men who worked there. Neither man is named in the preceding or following year's directory, leading one to speculate they may have been involved in a traveling tent-based skating enterprise, which was not uncommon in that day.

No fear—other rinks eventually cropped up around the city.

ALAMO ROLLER-SKATING RINK

When Cedar Rapids' first amusement park, the Alamo, opened on the west side of town in 1906, the roller-skating rink was a big draw. The smooth maple floor and the amusement park setting made it a popular destination. Proper attire and disciplined patrons were a requirement. But the park itself went downhill quickly, and after only seven years, the rink and the park closed.

AUDITORIUM SKATING RINK

From 1889 to 1969, there was a magnificent structure situated downtown, just off First Avenue, backing up to the river at 127 First Street NE, called the Auditorium. It was built by the Cedar Rapids Auditorium Company, whose officers were city leaders George Hedges, JF Allison, John Bever and George Lincoln, with city movers and shakers Greene and Forbes taking administrative roles just a few years later.

A two-story redbrick and white stone castle-looking structure with a towering dome above the entrance, it was near the place where Osgood Shepherd had built the first log cabin in the area fifty years earlier. Sometimes referred to as the City Auditorium and, in later years, as the Eagles Club, this grand building was situated between the Southern/Gorman Hotel/Riverside Inn to the south and the Peoples Theater to the north.

In those times, auditoriums were the centers for social activity, hosting entertainers, speakers, musicians, lectures, wedding dances and banquets. What else might one do with a large, open, flat-floored indoor room? Roller-skating!

Between the years 1909 and 1934, the Auditorium Skating Rink was *the* place to experience the turn-of-the-century roller-skating craze. As a fun and healthy pastime, skating was often chosen over dancing and other types of entertainment.

In 1935, the main function of the building was shifted from skating to dancing, the Pla-Mor Ballroom opened for business and roller-skaters found other places to skate.

WIGWAM ROLLER RINK

In 1932, another location for roller-skating had opened. The Wigwam was just south of the Marion city limits along the Boulevard, located at the Cedar Park outdoor facility. A six-thousand-square-foot hardwood floor was installed under the large semipermanent tent, and roller-skating enthusiasts had a new place to skate.

It lasted only a couple of summers, and eventually, an open-sided building replaced the tent, and the spot housed the Cedar Park Ballroom, which was later home to the Ce-Mar Acres Skating Rink.

TEMPLE ROLLER RINK

The El Kahir Shriner Temple was built in 1927 at 520 A Avenue NE. This impressive landmark high on the hill was home to a variety of Shriner activities and functions. But the Shriners quickly discovered that the cost to maintain the structure was excessive, and they sought out renters to share the space and help defray the costs.

By 1940, the Shriners had moved out, the main floor was rented out for skating and the Temple Roller Rink opened. It was immediately popular, and roller-skating was well-liked here for over thirteen years. Advertising for the rink proclaimed:

> *The First Sign of Spring—Little Children Roller Skating—go skating yourself!*
> *Skate for Health's Sake!*
> *Bring Your Date to Skate!*
> *Entertain Your Friends Here—Parties Arranged!*

Meanwhile, the Iowa National Guard had taken up residence in the temple, and in 1951 the National Guard bought the building, and it became known as the Shrine Armory.

In 1953, the skating-rink closed, and the guard expanded its indoor activities. By 1967, the entire building had been vacated, and soon after, due to structural concerns and in preparation for the coming I-380 project, it was torn down.

CE-MAR ACRES SKATING RINK

In 1944, the old Cedar Park, midway on the Cedar Rapids/Marion city line, was purchased by a couple who had spent several years setting up traveling roller-skating rinks in various small towns and were looking for a permanent home. The McElhinneys planned to develop the entire property into an outdoor amusement park, but the first thing they did was reopen the Cedar Park roller rink (the former Cedar Park Ballroom, originally the site of the Wigwam Roller Rink) and rename it Ce-Mar Acres Skating Rink.

Kids, adults and entire families loved to indulge in roller-skating at the Ce-Mar. In 1952, matinees cost thirty cents, and evening skating was only sixty cents. Roller-skating at Ce-Mar lasted twenty-four years, until the park and the rink permanently closed in 1968.

ARMAR ROLLER RINK

On December 26, 1964, the popular ballroom next door to Ce-Mar covered the dance floor with blue plastic and changed its name. Armar Roller Rink offered skating for a month before the new name was adjusted to Armar Roller Rink & Ballroom. That lasted four more months, until May 1965, when the blue floorcovering was removed, and roller-skating was discontinued. The venue's name reverted to Armar Ballroom, and its newspaper ads proclaimed its "return to dancing."

ROLLER DROME

A new roller-skating rink was built in Cedar Rapids in 1958. This was a big one. It was a domed airplane hangar–looking building three-fourths of a mile south of Hawkeye Downs at 5715 Sixth Street SW. Ads promoted it as:

> *Iowa's Largest Skating Floor, 3 to 4 times as Large as the Average Rink!*
> *Meet all your old friends that used to skate at the Temple Roller Rink!*
> *Tuesday Night, Buck Night—Whole Family for a Dollar!*
> *Police-Patrolled at All Times!*

Skaters enjoyed the facility for five years before it closed in the summer of 1961, becoming a temporary headquarters for the army reserve for a couple of years. Later, the building was an implement dealer, a Spra-White location, a furniture and appliance store, a truck service business, an auction barn and then Best Buy Floral Supply for a long time. Today, it's Brown Supply Company.

But before another decade passed, there were more "Roller Drome" skating rinks popping up.

The December 12, 1958 grand opening announcement of the first Roller Drome. *Courtesy of the* Gazette.

ROLLER DROME OF CEDAR RAPIDS

Two new indoor roller-skating rinks were built in the '60s, the first one going up just a year after the Roller Drome on Sixth Street closed. Both of these were also called Roller Dromes. The first one went up on the west side of Cedar Rapids, and four years later, another one opened in Marion.

To get to the Cedar Rapids Roller Drome location, which opened in 1962, you'd head west on Sixteenth Avenue. It was way out there, past the Twin Towers, past Edgewood Road, past Wiley Blvd and past West Post Road—keep going, you're almost there.

There it is on your left, at 5711 Sixteenth Avenue SW next to the Dog 'N Suds, directly in front of the Superkart Speedway go-cart track that was built a year later in 1963.

When the roller rink first opened, advertising in the *Gazette* noted, "Live Hammond Organ Music!" When the rink closed thirteen years later, in May 1976, the *Gazette* suggested, "The last skate…say you were there when it all ended!"

Later, that same building housed Cedar Rapids Honda & Yamaha before becoming Sperry Engines.

ROLLER DROME OF MARION

In 1966, another location opened, this time in Marion. Also named Roller Drome, this one was also a domed airplane hangar–looking building. To get to the Marion location, you'd go east on Seventh Avenue, turning south on Thirty-Fifth Street at Castle Lanes/Towns Edge Auto. Cross the

The Marion Roller Drome building today. *Author's collection.*

tracks into the new industrial park, and on your right, at 320 Thirty-Fifth Street, was the new Roller Drome of Marion. Kids skated, teens dated and young adults met and sometimes married, according to Facebook posts today.

In 1974, new owners changed the name to Marion Roller Rink, but it closed in 1975. Since then, the big domed building has been home to ReVosWel Lumber for over forty years.

SKATE COUNTRY

Skate Country, at 3233 Sixth Street SW, opened in 1973—the same time as its next-door bowling neighbor, Lancer Lanes. Ads in the Yellow Pages promoted Skate Country as:

> *The Place Where the Fun Times Roll*
> *One of the Finest Skating Complexes in the Nation*
> *Wholesome Family Recreation for All Ages*
> *Air-Conditioned Comfort*
> *Newest in Music Systems*
> *Unusual Lighting Effects*
> *Near Sound-Proof Floor*
> *Private Parties, and also*
> *Birthday Party Packages.*

After twenty-four years, the roller rink closed, and the building became the Country Club Night Club until 1999, when it was briefly Leisure Time Billiards & Sports Bar. The building is gone now.

SUPER SKATE

Today, there is only one skating rink left in Cedar Rapids. Super Skate opened more than forty years ago, in 1976, in a new building at 5100 Northland Avenue NE, not far from Lindale.

Rex Roeher had started in the roller-skating rink business thirty years earlier, offering traveling skating rinks in tents, before settling down in Cedar

Rapids and opening Super Skate. Eventually he turned over the operation to his daughter and her husband, Pam and Gary Hester.

Over the years, advertisements noted the many popular skating amenities at this fine facility, including super silent floor, adult supervision, singles skates, adults-only skates and New Year's Eve teen parties.

So, if you feel the urge to "travel on surfaces with roller skates," head over to Super Skate any Wednesday, Friday, Saturday or Sunday, and always remember, "Skate in the same direction as the other skaters."

5
AMUSEMENT PARKS

I feel that something should be built, some kind of family park where parents and children could have fun together. It will be something that will never be finished, something we can keep developing and adding to. And it will get better as we find out what the public likes.
—Walt Disney

Walt Disney was speaking about Disneyland, but he was also wisely describing how all amusement parks should be operated—safe, fun and inviting for families. Cedar Rapids had four such parks over the years, some of them enjoying many years of popularity, as they not only grew but also evolved with the public's constantly changing expectation of fun.

THE ALAMO

Alamo Park was Cedar Rapids' first amusement park. It was built on the west side of town in 1906, five years after Walt Disney's birth, and forty-five years before he began developing his vision of Disneyland. The Alamo had a short seven-year life. But at first, with the roller coaster, Ferris wheel, roller-skating rink and waterslide ride, the park was extremely popular. And the owners did keep developing and adding to it, though various issues sadly brought it to a quick demise.

The Alamo took up ten acres at Thirteenth Street NW between B and E Avenues, where Roosevelt Middle School now sits. The highly anticipated June 11, 1906 grand opening was given a full page in the *Republican*: "18 acres, beautifully illuminated with thousands of electric lights, wooded lawns, graveled plazas and paths. A superb place of legitimate recreation for respectable people. No gambling. Open Wednesday, Saturday and Sunday afternoons."

The grand opening featured concerts, live vaudeville shows, jugglers, and acrobats. Rides and amenities included a figure-eight roller coaster, 50 feet high and 1,550 feet long; a Shoot-the-Chutes waterslide ride; a 100-foot Ferris wheel; a merry-go-round; a roller-skating rink; a movie theater; a dance pavilion; a bicycle racetrack; hot-air balloon rides; target galleries; food and snacks; and benches, picnic areas, swings and playgrounds.

By 1909, new management was struggling with operational problems, and with the addition of gambling and alcoholic beverages, the park started getting rundown quickly. It felt like less of a family-friendly venue. Five acres of the property—the parade and circus grounds—were sold off to the new Cedar Rapids Baseball Association and became a baseball complex for the next decade.

The Alamo's last season was in 1913. The rides were sold, and the gates were locked, although the waterslide pond was occasionally used for ice skating in the wintertime.

The fence and remaining structures at the Alamo were torn down in 1921 to prepare for the construction of Roosevelt School.

FRONTIER PARK

Hawkeye Downs is the area's largest racetrack, fairgrounds, convention center and amphitheater for concerts. But when it was originally built in 1925 by the local Amusement Association, it was billed as "Frontier Park—Iowa's Largest Amusement Park."

Undeveloped property south of town at 4400 Sixth Street SW was purchased by the Cedar Rapids Amusement Association, and a racetrack and grandstand were built. Rodeos were popular at the time, and that first year, a rodeo event packed the grandstand with riding, roping, trick riding, a mounted band and a tribe of Native Americans camping in tepees along the track.

The ownership of the property changed hands from the original association to the chamber of commerce, then to the city and finally to a new association. But amusements were never developed, and the facility eventually changed its name and went on to become a popular racetrack and fairgrounds.

CE-MAR ACRES AMUSEMENT PARK

In 1944, Don and Clista McElhinney purchased the old Cedar Park property at 5001 First Avenue SE, as well as eighteen surrounding acres. They wanted to build a modern amusement park with a wide range of entertainment and offerings for adults and children. And they were successful.

Because the land covered parts of both Cedar Rapids and Marion, they gave their new facility the appropriate name of Ce-Mar Acres. On that piece of property was the Cedar Park Rink, formerly the Cedar Park Ballroom, and they quickly reopened the roller rink.

Two years later, in 1946, they opened a dirt racetrack and ran midget car races. The Midget Bowl Racetrack grew to become one of the most popular tracks in the country.

Carnivals and traveling midway shows had been setting up at Cedar Park for years, and the McElhinneys continued that tradition, at least initially, with a long-term goal of setting up permanent amusements onsite. They began by acquiring and installing children's rides.

By the summer of 1952, the amusement park was in full swing. Kiddie boat rides, chariots, swings, cars, a Ferris wheel and games, in addition to the racetrack and roller rink, made Ce-Mar a family destination. The park was open every evening and on weekend afternoons.

In 1954, the miniature train ride opened. Called the Hiawatha, it could carry thirty-six passengers and had lights, whistles and a bell and sounded just like a real train. With over 1,800 feet of track, it was the largest miniature railroad in Iowa.

A 1913 CW Parker carousel was added in 1957. Also called a merry-go-round, this one was populated with brightly painted horses, rabbits, a chariot and a love seat. Powered by a gasoline engine, the wooden horses were all handmade, and the reins were real leather. With a Wurlitzer air-operated roller organ, along with drums and whistles, the carousel was a delight for kids of all ages.

In 1958, a roller coaster was installed. With a pony ride, a Tilt-A-Whirl, carnival food and snacks, Ce-Mar was complete. By 1968, after twenty-four years of operation, the McElhinneys decided to close the park. The property and amusements were sold, the land was cleared and in 1984, a big Jack's Discount Store was built on the property. It eventually became a Shopko and then a series of other shops. Today it's the home of the M.A.C. fitness center.

CHAPMAN'S FUN WORLD

Gene Chapman had a background in golf—he had been a golf pro, managed various country clubs and owned a driving range. Originally from Wisconsin, he worked in Dubuque, Cedar Rapids and Iowa City before returning to Cedar Rapids to create his legacy.

In 1953, Gene, his wife and another couple opened Gene Chapman Sports on the southwest edge of town along Highway 151/Williams Boulevard. They built a driving range, an eighteen-hole miniature golf course and three batting cages. Gene was on hand to provide lessons on the driving range and was often asked to give golf tips on radio shows.

Renamed Chapman's Sports Center in 1958, a one-of-a-kind double-deck driving range was installed with ten tees situated on the upper level. It also added archery ranges and a par-three golf course that was open to the public and hosted various charity tournaments. Over the next couple of years, trampolines were added as well.

By 1962, it was operating under the name Chapman's Recreation Center. Highway widening removed part of the property and forced the owners to rearrange the miniature golf course and three holes of the larger one. Lights were soon added to the course, which brought extended hours and increased business. But the double-decker was closed due to the occasional ball being aimed at a golfer.

In 1969, a large building was added, providing an indoor driving range where balls were hit into huge nets. Three years later, the indoor driving range was removed, and indoor putt-putt replaced it and became a huge attraction.

In 1977, Gene sold the business to his daughter Andrea and her husband, Eddie Cole, who was a Big Ten and NCAA trampoline champion, a world champion high diver and an excellent golfer.

What else could be added? The next novelty was the huge waterslide that was installed in 1981. Climb the steps to the tall tower, go for a ride and come scooting out at the bottom. By 1989, Chapman Fun World was also offering go-carts and a kiddie roller coaster and other rides, but it closed the golf operation.

In September 2001, Chapman Fun World closed for the season and never reopened. The property was sold, and the land became the site for Williams Plaza, a shopping and business center at 3001 Williams Boulevard SW. The waterslide was donated and installed at the Vinton Parks & Recreation Swimming Pool.

6

RACETRACKS

The winner ain't the one with the fastest car, it's the one who refuses to lose.
—*Dale Earnhardt*

Nobody remembers who finished second but the guy who finished second.
—*Bobby Unser*

For forever, it seems, men have felt the need to race one another—not only footraces, but also with every form of transportation ever developed: automobile, motorcycle, boat, airplane. Way back in time, it was chariots. Around the time the young pioneer city of Cedar Rapids was developing, horse racing was the most popular form of competition. Oval-shaped tracks were created in open fields and lots. Spectators showed up in throngs to watch the horses and riders, or drivers, and their rigs sail around the track at breakneck speeds. Gradually, the races became organized, and the tracks were referred to as "driving parks."

The exact locations of the earliest Cedar Rapids area racetracks are lost, but the following are locations and descriptions of the five most recent tracks, including one still popular today.

DRIVING PARK

In 1886, when Cedar Rapids was still geographically small, Second and Third Avenues ended at about Fourteenth Street SE. That's where the Cedar Rapids Driving Park Association, founded by men with the names Greene and Bever, built this track.

It was a half-mile oval course with bleachers along one straightaway and a large grandstand along the other. Trotting and harness racing were widely promoted, and horse owners from all over the Midwest brought in their animals and drivers and two-wheeled sulkies. The infield was also used for traveling shows, carnivals, baseball games and fireworks displays.

One event in 1889 made the headlines—a champion trotter named Axtell came to town to race and attempt to break his own record. A city-wide reception was held, and a large delegation, including a band, met the train. The horse was welcomed with the presentation of a beautiful floral collar. Did he break his record? Sadly, the race results don't seem to exist today.

The last year for this park was 1892. New homes were in demand, and the area was ideal for neighborhoods. A new park was quickly built on the west side of town. Today, no traces remain of this old track.

DRIVING PARK

The next location was active from 1893 to 1908. Located at F and G Avenues between Ninth and Thirteenth Streets NW, it was described as being "at the west end of F." In this same area was the Athletic Park for baseball games, the Alamo Amusement Park for fun and entertainment and parade grounds for carnivals and outdoor gymnastic events. First Avenue West was widened, and new double-line trolley tracks were installed to handle the large volume of citizens headed to the parks on beautiful evenings and weekend days.

The driving park offered trotting and pacing meets promoted as "the greatest race meetings in Iowa," featuring "the best horses in the country."

Newspaper articles also noted that "the roof covering the bleachers, was not so much to offer protection from the sun and rain, but to block the dust and dirt from settling on the harness racing fans."

All of these entertainment parks and grounds closed or were relocated around the same time, and homes, churches and schools were soon built on those properties.

MARION INTERSTATE FAIR PARK

Meanwhile, the neighboring city of Marion had developed a large park called the Marion Interstate Fairgrounds & Racetrack. It was in use from 1901 to 1926. It was located along Indian Creek Road north of town.

The property had originally been farmland owned by Earl Granger, dating to 1856. It was a mile or so northeast of his classic brick homestead, which still exists as a museum. After the farmland was developed into a park, it was popular for racing and fairs, with huge covered grandstands and other amenities for the public.

As racing fell out of favor, the property was converted into a golf course. Originally called the Marion Country Club from 1926 to 1945, it has been home to the Indian Creek Country Club since 1946.

From the air, you can still see a vague outline of where the oval track was situated.

CE-MAR MIDGET BOWL

In 1944, Don McElhinney and his wife, Clista, purchased the old Cedar Park property along First Avenue and renamed it Ce-Mar Acres. In 1946 they built a fifth-mile oval dirt track on the rear of the property and named it Ce-Mar Bowl. It was located directly behind the Armar Ballroom, which wasn't built until two years later by separate owners.

Racing enthusiast Kyle Ealy has thoroughly documented the racetrack, and the following information is provided courtesy of the *Midwest Racing Archives*:

> *Running primarily midget cars on the small track, it immediately became a hit with drivers and fans alike, producing lightning-fast speeds and some of the closest side-by-side racing action in the area. Advertised as "The Fastest Cars in the Midwest," it drew skilled drivers from all over the Midwest. "This was the hotbed of midget racing," Hall of Famer Buzz Rose would say. "There was a lot of midget racing in its heyday, and the best drivers always raced at Ce-Mar."*
>
> *On Sunday mornings, you went to church. On Sunday evenings, you went to Ce-Mar Bowl to watch the midgets compete. Admission was $1.25 to "one of the biggest tracks in the country." Night midget racing was introduced in 1947 after the addition of more than 30 light poles for illumination.*

MIDGET AUTO RACES

SUNDAY NIGHT

at

CE-MAR ACRES
DUSTLESS TRACK

Time Trials 7 P. M.   Races Start 8:15 P. M.

Races Every Sunday
Night Until Fall

'The Fastest Cars in the Midwest'

Ce-Mar racetrack ad from 1949 in the Cedar Rapids *Gazette*. *Courtesy of the* Gazette.

It became such a popular venue so quickly that in 1948, McElhinney would have to add more bleachers (2,000 more seats) to accommodate the overflow crowds. When the new seating was in place, 6,000 race fans could enjoy midget racing at Ce-Mar.

At the end of the '48 season, McElhinney announced that the racing surface, which had been clay since its opening, would be replaced with good ol' Eastern Iowa black dirt. McElhinney was convinced that as fast as the midgets toured his track on clay, the black dirt would make them go even faster.

Some say that McElhinney's eventual decision to run jalopies and stock cars instead of just midgets was the reason for the track's downfall. But things change, and competing against the bigger and more modern Hawkeye Downs Speedway across town became a struggle, and race fan crowds became smaller and smaller as the years passed. Finally, in 1955, the track was shut down for good.

The property was eventually sold and redeveloped into a Jack's Discount Store location, which later became a Shopko, and today is home to The M.A.C fitness club. And opening in 2017, in the north end of that large building, in the old Hancock Fabric store was an indoor go-cart track called Speedeezz Indoor Karting. Which amazingly happened to be sitting directly on top of the old Ce-Mar Bowl racetrack.

FRONTIER PARK/HAWKEYE DOWNS SPEEDWAY

Fourteen years after the first Indianapolis 500 automobile race was held, Cedar Rapids built its own racetrack called Frontier Park on Sixth Street SW. It opened in 1925, with a dirt track and a grandstand that could seat thirteen thousand race fans. Although the park was available for carnivals, fairs, rodeos, livestock shows and other exhibitions, its strength has always been in car racing. Horse races and motorcycle races were also presented during some of the earlier years.

The venue's name changed briefly, and it was called the Cedar Rapids Speedway from 1932 to 1935. But in 1936, it was given its permanent name, Hawkeye Downs.

The oval-shaped racetrack, with its two five-hundred-foot-long straightaways, is a half-mile loop. In 1950, a second, internal fourth-mile track was added for midget car races and demolition derbies.

The track's reputation grew, attracting great racers from all over the country. In 1966, the old wooden grandstand was replaced with a modern concrete and steel structure, which still stands today. The huge canopied center section is flanked by two large open-air seating sections, with concessions under the main section.

In 1989, the decision was made to move beyond dirt, and both the half- and fourth-mile tracks were converted to asphalt. Further enhancements developed shortly, including paved pits, an enclosed tech building, high-quality lighting and an electronic message board. More recent improvements include a Daktronics scoreboard and message center, plus a transponder timing and scoring system.

Considered one of the premier tracks in the Midwest, Hawkeye Downs has long been a popular venue for outdoor family entertainment. Today, under new ownership, it remains an important destination for regional and national series races, including the American Speed Association, the International Motor Contest Association, NASCAR, the United Midget Auto Racing Association, the United States Auto Club and the American Indy Car Series.

GO-CART TRACKS

Over the years, go-cart racing has been a fun pastime for adults and kids. The various indoor and outdoor tracks were never around very long, but they were fun while they lasted.

The following are the outdoor tracks from the area:

Hawkeye Downs: Go-carts (1959)
Superkart Speedway: Behind Roller Drome and Dog 'N Suds, west on Highway 30 (1963–72)
Cecil Reed's Sepia Quarter Midget Track: On Mount Vernon Road (1960s)
Marion: Towns Edge Shopping Center had a track in the parking lot

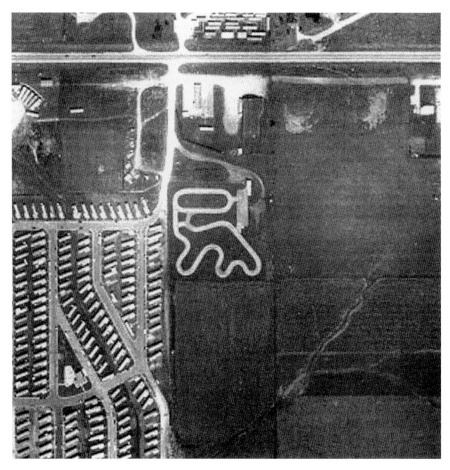

A 1966 aerial view of Superkart Speedway go-cart track behind the Roller Drome and Dog 'N Suds on Highway 30 West. *Courtesy of ISU GIS Support and Research Facility.*

Chapman's Fun World: On Williams Boulevard (1980s and '90s)
Speedy D's: In the Westdale Mall parking lot behind JC Penney (mid-1990s)

The following are the indoor tracks:

Formula Fun: In the old Van Meter building, 240 Thirty-Third Avenue SW (2003–06)
Speedeezz Indoor Karting: Old Hancock Fabrics/old Ce-Mar location (2017–18) 1120 Thirty-Third Avenue SW (2019)

OTHER RACETRACKS

Don & Al's Family Raceway had slot car racing. It was located at 3140 Sixteenth Avenue SW in 1966–67. And, of course, the Speedway Lounge Bar & Grill was at 706 Second Avenue SE in 1983. It offered bar stool races.

7

SPORTS TEAMS

Being a sports fan is a complex matter, in part irrational but not unworthy; a relief from the seriousness of the real world, with its unending pressures and often grave obligations.
—Richard Gilman

I believe God created sports for a good reason. It's recreation. It's something that we enjoy. It teaches us a lot as well....I believe God is a sports fan.
—Luke Scott

We all like watching sports—some more than others. We like watching our kids play, we like high school athletics and we *love* our Iowa college sports teams. When it comes to professional sports, Cedar Rapids may not be a big enough city to support its own major league teams, but we've had a bountiful supply of minor league, semipro and junior league teams. The following are lists of these popular sporting organizations. Some of these teams are still around, though most are long gone. Have you ever seen any of these teams play?

BASEBALL:
Kernels (1993–present)
Reds (1980–92)
Giants (1975–79)
Astros (1973–74)

Cardinals (1965–72)
Red Raiders (1963–64)
Braves (1958–62)
Raiders (1954–57)
Indians (1950–53)
Rockets (1948–49)
No team due to World War II (1942–48)
Raiders (1934–42)
Bunnies (1913–32)
No team (1910–12)
Rabbits (1896–09)
Canaries (1890–95)

BASKETBALL:
Running Guns: American Basketball Association (2007)
Ball Hogs: All-American Professional Basketball League (2005)
River Raiders: Unite States Basketball League (2004)
Unicorns: Women's Basketball Association (1993–94)
Sharpshooters: Global Basketball Association (1992–93)
Silver Bullets: Continental Basketball Association (1988–91)
Cornets: Women's Professional Basketball League (1978–81)

FOOTBALL:
River Kings: Indoor Football League (2019–present)
Titans (2012–18)
Raiders (1998–99)
Falcons (1976–78)
Bucs (1974)
Rapid Raiders (1972–73)
Crushers (1936–38)

HOCKEY:
Rough Riders: United States Hockey League (1999–present)

SOCCER:
Inferno: Midwest Premier League (2019)
Rampage United: Premier League of America (2016–17)
Rampage: Major Arena Soccer (2015–18)

PART II

———————————— ℮ℓℓ ————————————

DISTRICTS

8

CZECH VILLAGE

I was born in America, but all of my friends' parents, everybody's parents, including my own, had come to America from Europe. Many people in my neighborhood hardly bothered to learn English.
—*Christopher Walken*

Cedar Rapids has a large Czech population, with close to 20 percent of our citizens having some Czech heritage in their blood. The original Bohemian settlers who came to Linn County began arriving in the 1860s. Immigrants were attracted to this area after hearing about available farmland and plentiful industrial, meat packing and other jobs.

An Irishman can be somewhat credited for Cedar Rapids' large Czech population. Thomas Sinclair opened his packinghouse, T.M. Sinclair & Co., in 1871. Originally located downtown on Third Avenue (around where the Montrose Hotel was later built), he soon found a location on the south edge of town. He hired some of the Bohemians in the area and found their work ethic second to none. Sinclair encouraged his employees to urge family and friends back home to come to the United States and Cedar Rapids and to let them know they had jobs waiting for them. Many villages in Bohemia thinned out as families crossed the ocean and headed for the States.

Eventually, Czech Village developed to serve the immigrant population that was building homes on the west side of the river. The small business district on Sixteenth Avenue SW consisted of meat markets, grocers, tailors, blacksmiths and everything else you would find in a small town.

Mural on a wall along C Street SW in Czech Village. *Photo by Peter D. Looney.*

But with the passing of time and the decline of heavy industry in Cedar Rapids, as well the aging of the immigrant population, this commercial district began to deteriorate. In the early '70s, the remaining Czech business owners and others proud of their Czech ancestry began an effort to revitalize the area. The charming little Czech Village was reborn. Today, shops and restaurants populate every building on the avenue. Proud descendants gladly share their rich culture and heritage with their friends and neighbors. With the revitalization of the original business district, this fascinating old-world heritage is preserved.

9

NEW BOHEMIAN DISTRICT/NEWBO

I grew up in an immigrant neighborhood.
We just knew the rule was you're going to have to work twice as hard.
—*Lin-Manuel Miranda*

As the young city of Cedar Rapids grew, industrial areas were built up along the Fourth Street railroad corridor. By the late 1800s, the southeast side was an agricultural and manufacturing hub, home to factories, warehouses, foundries, bottlers and meat packers.

The New Bohemia area on south Third Street was home for the large Czech and Slovak communities that settled in Cedar Rapids to work both here and throughout the city. Homes and neighborhoods sprang up alongside a fast-growing mixture of shops and businesses. Social halls, theaters, cafés, taverns, pool halls, grocery stores, banks and churches—the area was its own little community.

Over time, changes in the economy resulted in many of these businesses closing; however, this part of the city has clung to its cultural and entrepreneurial identity.

Today, this district is a vibrant urban neighborhood model for historic preservation and economic development, and it is a destination for both residents and visitors. It has become a dynamic arts and culture center that provides unique shopping and dining opportunities. NewBo City Market, built in the structure of an old iron foundry, is home to one-of-a-kind food and retail start-ups; farmers' and artisan markets; and numerous community arts, entertainment and educational events. As a gathering place, business incubator and event center, the City Market services needs for a wide spectrum of people and organizations.

NewBo has become a dynamic public space, promoting health, happiness and well-being.

10

LITTLE MEXICO

The American dream comes from opportunity. The opportunity comes from our founding principles, our core values that are held together and protected by the Constitution. Those ideas are neither Republican, Democrat, conservative, liberal, white, or black. Those are American ideologies.
—*Ted Yoho*

From 1910 to 1970, there was a cultural district just north of downtown Cedar Rapids, populated predominantly by the Mexican American community and referred to as Little Mexico. Abutting the tracks and Cedar Lake, with the train yards and Cargill to the west and St. Luke's on the east, there were ten square blocks of houses in an area along B and C Avenues NE between Fifth and Eighth Streets.

In the early 1900s, many Mexican men immigrated to the United States to work on the railroads, and many settled in Cedar Rapids. In those days, it was common for the railroad companies to provide old boxcars and shacks for the workers and their families to live in temporarily. It was not the ideal environment, but hard workers had opportunities to improve their situation.

By and large, the men were dependable, and the steady income allowed them to purchase homes in the area that had been the houses of the brewery workers of the previous generation. The families took pride in their accomplishments, and it showed in their neat neighborhoods.

Unfortunately, progress was looming in the form of an interstate highway, which would pass directly through the area. Also, some of the properties were showing their age. Between 1967 and 1970, the residents dispersed and relocated, over one hundred buildings were removed and the land was cleared. Today, the S-curves of the busy, six-lane I-380 pass over the Little Mexico area.

But back in the day, the residents enjoyed their neighborhood, as former resident James J. Vasquez recalls in *A Young Boy's Memories*:

> *For me it was the perfect place to grow up, because it was three blocks from downtown, four blocks from the Cedar River and three blocks from the Cedar Lake slough. Every Saturday some of the kids from the neighborhood and I would get a quarter from our parents and go downtown and decide which of the five movie theaters to go to, the Paramount, the State, the Town, the Palace or the Iowa Theater. Summers at Whittam Park were spent full of fun activities. We played games, got wet in the wading pool and competed with the other Cedar Rapids parks in sport events. One of my happiest memories was in 1960. The Whittam Park softball team, which I was a member, finished second place in the Cedar Rapids parks softball tournament. Other memories included walking to the Cedar River dam with my brother, cousins, and friends to go fishing. We spent time at the Cedar Lake slough floating on wooden rafts and truck inner tubes. We chased rabbits along the railroad tracks and found frogs along the Cedar Lake. These were all fond memories and were places all within walking distance for a young boy growing up in the area known as Little Mexico.*

11

TIME CHECK

I grew up in a working-class neighborhood,
so there was always a sense of struggle, but we had hope.
—*Bonnie Hunt*

On the west side, across the river from Quaker Oats, was a big area of small homes that has been called the Time Check District for over one hundred years. Generally bordered by F Avenue on the south, Ellis Park on the north, Ellis Boulevard on the west and the river on the east, it's a flat, low-lying area that is barely elevated above the river level.

In the late 1800s, houses and neighborhoods popped up, many of them home to workers in the railroad yards across the river. When the railroad companies would have an occasional payroll financial situation, they would give the crew postdated paychecks. Banks would let workers cash these checks in advance of posted dates, allowing the workers to pay bills and cover their expenses, and the banks would delay the railroad's obligation.

These become known as "time checks," and gradually, the term was used to describe the neighborhood as a whole. The excellent employment relationship between the residents and the railroad continued for many years, and as the railroads diminished, the Quaker Oats plant provided many residents with new jobs and the ability to remain in the neighborhood.

The blue-collar nature of the Time Check neighborhood ensured its longevity, but by the '90s, the neighborhood began experiencing an aging infrastructure and residential base, as well as other challenges typically faced by historic districts.

And then the flood hit. Time Check lost the vast majority of single-family homes and rental units to the devastating 2008 floodwaters. As part of the cleanup, they've all been removed, along with the old concrete streets and utilities above and underground. Planning continues, and it's likely that the space will continue into the future as a green space and part of the city's flood control area.

12

MOUNT VERNON ROAD

*We live in a world that has narrowed into a neighborhood
before it has broadened into a brotherhood.*
—*Lyndon B. Johnson*

Not necessarily a district, the Mount Vernon Road area is a unique section of Cedar Rapids with interesting and historical features. Originating at the Cedar River at Eighth Avenue SE, the road angles northeast until it reaches Mercy Hospital and Tenth Street, where the direction shifts slightly. The street then heads east and is now called Mount Vernon Road. Continue following it directly east through town and then out of town, go about 10 more miles and you'll eventually come to Mount Vernon.

You probably know that the earliest coast-to-coast transcontinental highway across the United States was designated in the early 1900s and was called the Lincoln Highway. In this area, it originally came through Mount Vernon, headed northwest to Marion and then southwest into Cedar Rapids via First Avenue, which was then called Marion Boulevard. In 1922, the Lincoln Highway route was shifted to bypass Marion and entered Cedar Rapids directly from the east on Mount Vernon Road.

Back then, the road was curvy, but as time passed, it evolved. Hills were removed, new bridges were built and the road was straightened. Yet history remains, including an old section of the original concrete, some of the old buildings and bullet holes left behind by such visitors as Al Capone and John Dillinger—more on that later.

The following is a short list of some of the interesting places along Mount Vernon Road, with street addresses abbreviated to "MVR SE." This list begins near Mercy Hospital and continues east.

Sam's Pizza: Carryout pizza at 1052 MVR SE, just past the Tenth Street intersection (1977–83); relocated to 2874 MVR SE (1986–97).

Ambroz Recreation Center: 2000 MVR SE, formerly the old Buchanan School building (1903–73); now an office of the Cedar Rapids Parks and Recreation Department.

Sun Mart: The second of several Sun Marts built by Nash Finch in Cedar Rapids, 2405 MVR SE (1953–70); later in the '70s, it was a MeToo Supermarket, and now a Goodwill store is located there.

The Vernon Inn: The original location was 2706 MVR SE (1970s–90s); it then moved across the street. The original two-story redbrick building, torn down in the early 2000s, had been home to a fun assortment of eating and drinking establishments, including Backstairs Lounge (1997), Eddie Piccard Jazz Club (1994–99), Greek Islands (1992–93), Inn Pasta (1990), Vernon Inn 1976–88), Ye Olde Vernon Inn (1970–76), Charlie's Pizza (1963), Stop in Tavern (1951–63), Clyde Zedick Tavern (1947), Kubicek's (1950), Walt Workman's Tavern (1940–45), Herbert Tavern (1939), the Canteen (1936) and Lincoln Nite Club (1933).

The sturdy Buchanan School building as it stands today. *Photo by Peter D. Looney.*

Vernon Inn, the Greek Place: The second location was across the road at 2663 MVR SE (1990–2015), in the old Family Tree Restaurant (1983–88), the Chicken Shoppe (1979–80) and a Texaco gas station (1960s–70s). This building was recently removed, and a new O'Reilly Auto Parts store is now there.

Hy-Vee: Originally at 2711 MVR SE at the Memorial Drive intersection, until the company built a Hy-Vee Superstore at 4035 MVR SE in 1997. The old location later became a Sun Mart and is home to a CVS Pharmacy today.

Lincolnway Court Cabins: 2734 MVR SE, a block or so east of the original Vernon Inn, where All Saints School is now. Back in the day, when travelers and tourists passed through town and needed to stop for the night, the downtown area offered a multitude of restaurants and hotel accommodations that were convenient for train passengers. However, traveling motorists soon became aware of the inconvenience and expense of bringing a car into the heart of the city for an overnight stay. So, cabin camps opened on the edges of town—the forerunners of today's motels. One of several camps along the east edge of town, the Lincolnway, was in operation from 1930 to the 1950s.

Cork N Fork: A tasty little restaurant at 2835 MVR SE (1980–2013).

The Best Showboat: A night club at 3102 MVR SE (1934). Before that it had been the Rhythm Club, closing in 1933. Later on, it was a service station, an auto repair shop and various barbecue restaurants, including Little Pigs of America, Little Bob's Barbeque and Bar-B-Que Delight, all in the 1960s. From 1973 to the present, it has been Kings Gard and now City Wide Cleaners.

King's Food Host: 3414 MVR SE, it's the "Home of the Cheese Frenchee! Phone in Your Order from your Booth!" (1970–75). Today, it is a Community Savings Bank.

DW Dawg: "The Original D.W Butter-Dipped Dawg in a Sesame Bun," this was one of three locations in Cedar Rapids. This one was at 3531 MVR SE (1982–83). It then became a Happy Joe's and is now Croissant Du Jour.

Leonardo's: At 4061 MVR SE (1975–83). A popular Cedar Rapids pizza joint, there's still a location on Sixteenth Avenue SW. After this Mount Vernon Road location closed, it was Luenzi's from 1988–94. Later, it was Rooster's Bar & Grill, from 1997–98. The building was torn down when the Hy-Vee Superstore was built behind it, and the corner restaurant property has now been vacant for twenty years.

Continue east on Mount Vernon Road, past that new Hy-Vee, past the water tower and you're on the top of the hill. Keep going, up ahead is a section of businesses on your left, on the north side of the road. The following are some of the interesting ones:

Country Corner Western Wear: At 4398 MVR SE, for boots and leather and all kinds of cowboy stuff. In 2017, a home furnishings business called Industry Fashions moved into the back section. Back in the 1960s this building was home to Ace Furniture Mart.

Melvin Brunskill Restaurant & Gas: At 4550 MVR SE (1939–47); became Olive's Truck Stop in the 1950s.

Meffords Auto Repair: At 4580 MVR SE for over thirty years. But way before that, the Wee Blue Inn was located here from 1933–46.

These next Mount Vernon Road businesses are on the right, farther down, on the south side of the road:

Louie Trombino's Roman Inn: "Just before Indian Creek" in the old Rosedale School building at 5977 MVR SE from 1953–54, following Club 30. A big Knights of Columbus Hall was built there in 1978. In 2001, A Touch of Class banquet hall and convention center took over the building and the property and remains there today.

Motel Sepia: At 6001 MVR SE, this was opened by Cecil and Evelyn Reed in 1953. Motels that would welcome black people during the early 1950s could be difficult to find, so the Reeds took advantage of owning undeveloped property on the Lincoln Highway and built a motel that was open to all. They also had added a kids' park and a small racetrack to the property. The Sepia Motel is discussed in further detail in Part VI.

Lighthouse Inn: At 6907 MVR SE. Built in 1912, the Lighthouse Inn was originally a small restaurant where you could enjoy dinner and drinks and maybe rent one of the cabins that used to sit behind the restaurant. According to the owners, "During Prohibition it became a common stop for Chicagoland mobsters looking to 'beat the heat' until things cooled off back in the Windy City. Yes, Al Capone did dine here. As did John Dillinger. If you're sitting in the booth to the left of the lounge entrance, that's exactly where his gun went off and left a hole in the wall. No longer there, but it's still a part of our history." The Lighthouse continues to serve fine dining today and is one of the oldest operating businesses in Cedar Rapids.

WENDY OAKS TRAIN SPECIAL!

BRING THE FAMILY!
See the Miniature Train with Longest Track in the world which brings the food directly to the customer.
The Children will be Delighted!

SUNDAY SPECIAL — YOUR CHOICE

HICKORY SMOKED
BARBECUED RIBS
SMORGASBORD
DELICIOUS FILLET

$**1**50

WALLEYE PIKE
SMORGASBORD

Open Every Night Except Mondays 5 to 12 p.m.
Sundays, Noon to 9 p.m.

WENDY OAKS SUPPER CLUB
MT. VERNON ROAD SE

A unique way to have your food served at the Wendy Oaks Supper Club, according to this ad in the May 24, 1958 Cedar Rapids *Gazette. Courtesy of the* Gazette.

Just past the Lighthouse were three small buildings that were home to many dining and drinking establishments that came and went over the years. The most popular was certainly Wendy Oaks Supper Club, situated right next door to the Lighthouse, serving excellent meals from 1952 to 1960, before relocating to Springville. Others, with much shorter lifespans, included Coyotes Bar, Internet & Brew, Chubby's Bar & Grill, Club 6909, the Rut, Nancy's Bar & Grill, Nancy's Country Inn, Marty's Country Inn, Squaw Creek Tap, the Rebel Lounge and the Gamecock Inn. Wendy Oaks even came back for a while. Today, the only remaining building is on the lot of the old Belmont Grocery, and is home to Edith Lucielle's Bait Shack & Wing Depot, which opened in 2016.

PART III

LANDMARKS

13

MAY'S ISLAND AND CITY HALL

Located in the heart of Paris, on an island in the Seine River called Ile de la Cité ["City Island"], is the Palais de Justice. This massive home of French legislative power is an elegant complex of buildings that house France's judicial offices. It is also inextricably bound up with the history of royalty, as the palace was for a long time the residence of kings, who had all the legislative and executive power, as well as judicial authority.
—Paris Convention and Visitors Bureau.

Two major cities share the unique trait of housing their government offices on islands: Paris, France and Cedar Rapids, Iowa.
—Cedar Rapids Visitors and Convention Bureau

MAY'S ISLAND

May's Island is located in the middle of a wide spot in the Cedar River, just south of the rock-bottomed rapids where pioneers used to ford on their journeys west. The rocky, hilly, cedar-covered island eventually became the base of ferries and bridges crossing the river. Streets and homes and stores and even a factory made their way onto the island, until the 1910s, when the city bought the island, enlarged it and eventually built new government offices there.

The city renamed it Municipal Island, but that designation has pretty much disappeared. There is no signage on the island, and to this day, it continues to be referred to as May's Island.

In 2008, it was a flooded island. On June 13 of that year, the Cedar River crested at an unbelievable nineteen feet above flood level, more than eleven feet above the previous record. As Mike Goldberg, the administrative services director for Linn County so accurately stated, "Well, the island is part of the river now." But the waters eventually receded, the cleanup began and the business of running a city continues.

The following is a timeline of the island's colorful history:

1837: Legend has it that the area's first settler and notorious rabble-rouser Osgood Shepherd hides stolen horses on the island.

1860: Colonel John M. May officially purchases the island for the whopping fee of $7.50 and names it the Town of May Island.

1860: Through the early 1900s, May's Island had houses, businesses, a public pavilion and even a roller coaster—a wooden figure-eight contraption that was suspended from the trees.

1871: A free bridge is built, crossing May's Island at Third Avenue.

1904: Colonel May dies.

1904: The Fourth Avenue interurban rail bridges are built.

1905: The Second Avenue bridge is built. A cement bridge with railings, it crosses the north end of the island.

1910: The city purchases May's Island—all property, homes and businesses— for a total expenditure of $105,000, renames it Municipal Island and moves the city offices into the old Smulekoff's Island Store.

1925: A jail is built on the south end of the island.

1926: The Linn County Courthouse is built just north of the jail.

1927: Tons of dirt and rock are brought in and the island is extended to First Avenue. The City Hall/Veteran's Memorial Coliseum is built.

1953: Usage of the Fourth Avenue tracks is discontinued.

1960: An underground parking lot is built between Second and Third Avenues.

1964: A large parking lot is built behind the jail at the south tip of the island.

1966: The Fourth Avenue rail bridges are removed.

1983: A new Linn County Jail is built.

2008: The Cedar River flood severely damages all three buildings on the island.

CITY HALL

The three-story Empire House hotel was built in 1854 at 201 Third Avenue SE. The city immediately began renting rooms in it to manage the city's business. In 1869, an addition was added to the Empire, and new owners soon renamed the facility Park Avenue Hotel. (That was back when Third Avenue was called Park Avenue.) In 1876, the building was sold to the City of Cedar Rapids and officially became the city hall, where it housed city offices for more than thirty years.

In 1919, Linn County citizens voted to switch the county seat from Marion to Cedar Rapids. The city had already bought all of the properties on the island, and in an effort to unite the east side and the west side, the city offices moved onto the island in the old three-story Smulekoff's building, and officials tore down everything else on the island. They soon started bringing in ton after ton of fill dirt to extend the north end of the island from where it had ended just past Second Avenue and built it up all the way to First Avenue. They built the jail on the south end in 1925 and the Linn County Courthouse in 1926. They built the city hall/Veterans Memorial Coliseum in 1927 on the new extension. Then, they moved in and tore down the old Smulekoff's in 1928.

The city hall/veterans building is nationally recognized for its two-story stained-glass window designed by famed Iowa artist Grant Wood. On top of the building, a towering cenotaph represents the original Tomb of the Unknown Soldier at Arlington National Cemetery, topped with a faux eternal flame.

The following is a timeline of Cedar Rapids City Hall locations:

1854: Rent rooms in the Empire House at 201 Third Avenue SE
1870: Continue to rent the same rooms in the newly renamed Park Avenue Hotel
1876: Purchase the building, filling it with city leadership, judicial and service departments
1890: Expand city service departments into an additional building at 51 Second Street SE
1909: Purchase May's Island, including all of the private property, homes and businesses
1910: Move offices into the former Smulekoff's building on the island
1920: Remove all other buildings
1926: Build the Linn County Courthouse
1927: Build Veteran's Memorial Coliseum/city hall on Municipal Island
2008: Flooding Cedar River forces the evacuation and relocation of the city offices to temporary locations

14

HUNTER'S AIRPORT

The air up there in the clouds is very pure and fine, bracing and delicious.
And why shouldn't it be? It's the same air the angels breathe.
—Mark Twain

In 1903, near Kitty Hawk, North Carolina, two former Cedar Rapids boys invented and successfully flew the first sustained flight of an aircraft. The era of aviation had begun. Across the country, airfields were soon being built. According to the International Civil Aviation Organization, an airfield is "a defined area on land or water intended to be used either wholly or in part for the arrival, departure, and surface movement of aircraft." Add a hanger and buildings for staff, controllers, cargo and passengers, and you've got an airport.

Early airfields were equipped with grass or dirt runways, and they were not pleasant places for the passengers or fascinated observers. Arriving and departing aircraft blasted dirt, pebbles and grit into the bystanders' faces. On rainy days, they were mudholes. Many new airfields were created specifically for the new airmail system that was rapidly developing in the United States.

In the 1920s, when air flight was still in its infancy, World War I veteran and pilot Dan Hunter returned home to Cedar Rapids with a goal of creating a proper airport. He soon found 110 acres of flat, city-owned land south of town at the intersection of Bowling Street and Highway 30. The City of Cedar Rapids agreed with Hunter's suggestion and developed the

A souvenir flight certificate from a passenger's first flight in 1928. *Courtesy of Robert Thorpe and Karen Spicer Thorpe.*

four intertwined airstrips, originally naming it Cedar Rapids Airways and later changing it to Cedar Rapids Municipal Airport.

Dan Hunter barnstormed, transported passengers, managed the airport and taught flying lessons. In 1928, the airport became part of the nation's airmail service.

Hunter gave many people opportunities for their first plane rides. The following discussion is from an April 14, 2018 post on the Facebook page You Grew Up in Cedar Rapids in the '50s and '60s.

> *Robert Thorpe: My father-in-law, Lester Spicer got this souvenir certificate when he took a plane ride out at Hunter Airport. Notice that the airport stamped it with an official seal in the lower right: May 23, 1928.*
>
> *Karen Spicer Thorpe: That was my dad—he was just 22 years old at the time of this flight. I can just imagine how exciting this was for him as a young man.*
>
> *Comments: Thank you, what a great piece of history, I went by Hunter a lot as a child.*
>
> *Comments: I flew from Hunter Airport to East Moline and back, in Robert Armstrong's Stinson 4 passenger plane. He was my 8th grade Sunday school teacher, and if you had 100% attendance you got to fly with him.*

Comments: I used to fly out of Hunter Airport with my dad in a Piper Cub. Good memories.

Comments: My dad briefly flew for Hunter. In the early '50s, I think.

Comments: Hunter's was the first, and perhaps the only time I've seen the Goodyear blimp moored in Cedar Rapids.

In the late 1930s, at the onset of World War II, Coe College participated in a pilot training program called War Training Service. The program was based at the city's airfield and grew to seventy instructors and three hundred students.

Eventually, a new airport was built a few miles southwest to accommodate the newer, larger airplanes and jets. Today, it is called Eastern Iowa Airport, and it is on a street now named Wright Brothers Boulevard. Hunter's Airfield closed, and the land was sold in 1958, becoming an industrial park and housing businesses such as Midland Forge and the *Gazette*'s Color Web printing facility.

15

TRAIN DEPOTS

They say life is a journey, taken on a train,
With a pair of travelers, at each windowpane.
I may sit beside you, all the journey through,
Or I may sit elsewhere, never knowing you.
But if fate would allow me, to sit by your side,
Let's be pleasant travelers; it's so short a ride.
—Anonymous

My grandpa once told me that life is like a train. There are many stops along the
journey. Places you can get off, get refreshed, meet new people…
—sarahontheroad.com

All aboard!
—Every train conductor, everywhere

Iowa is an average-size state. Of all fifty states, Iowa is the twenty-sixth largest by square miles. It measures 310 miles wide, from Illinois to Nebraska, and is 200 miles "tall" from Minnesota to Missouri. That's quite a bit of land to cover when you're moving people and goods. So, from the mid-1800s to the mid-1900s, miles and miles of track were laid across Iowa. At one point, Iowa was the fifth-largest rail-mileage state in the country. A lot of trains moved a lot of people and goods, and a lot of depots were needed for the loading and unloading.

After tracks were laid, the first train pulled into town on June 15, 1859. Cedar Rapids is noteworthy because of the large amount of industry and grain processing, and several railroads quickly converged here. From the 1860s to the 1890s, Cedar Rapids was the state's leading rail hub.

In those days, the depot was often the economic and social focal point of the community it served. Marion had a large passenger and freight depot, and there were two large depots in downtown Cedar Rapids—the massive Union Station and the stately Rock Island Depot. Other smaller depots in town included interurban stations, freight depots, warehouse docks, factory docks and trolley barns. There were also rail yards and roundhouses.

Today, Cedar Rapids is home to three short line railroads: the Iowa Northern Railway, Iowa Interstate/Rock Island and the CRANDIC. Two Class 1 railroads service the city as well—the Canadian National and the Union Pacific, which manages the tracks and the crossings downtown. A small Rock Island/Chicago & Northwestern/Union Pacific freight depot is tucked into the remaining rail yards in the 400 block of Fourth Street NE.

The other depots are gone now. However, in Marion, the roof and bricks of the one-hundred-year-old Milwaukee Road depot were salvaged, moved a block west to the City Park and rebuilt into a large, useful public pavilion.

The following are some portraits of the lost depots of Cedar Rapids.

UNION STATION

A joint venture of the Chicago & Northwestern and the Burlington, Cedar Rapids & Northern railroads resulted in the creation of the magnificent Union Station. The original downtown train depots were on the northwest corner of First Avenue to A Avenue on the Fourth Street tracks, but were inelegant and did not represent the city very well to travelers and businesspeople.

The new Union Station was built in 1897 and was located on the Fourth Street rail corridor. It was an entire two blocks long between Third and Fifth Avenues SE, blocking off Fourth Avenue, and was situated on the west side of the tracks. The front of the depot faced downtown, with the front door on Fourth Avenue. The "business side" faced east, and right across the eleven sets of tracks were Greene Square Park as well as the old Washington High School, which replaced later by the Legion Lanes building and, even later, the city's new library.

The central portion of the redbrick building was trimmed in limestone and was 40 by 400 feet. There were 500-foot-long canopies along the tracks. The structure had an imposing 102-foot-high central tower, with a cupola that was removed in the 1950s.

Union Station's interior impressed travelers with its marble floors, high ceilings, oak paneling and brass railings. Two huge fireplaces with oak mantels anchored each end. It had its own lunch counter, which was often busy twenty-four hours a day.

At peak usage, the depot was capable of accommodating fifty passenger trains daily. But as highways were improved, cars, trucks and buses started becoming the preferred method of transportation, and in the 1930s, rail service began declining. By the late '50s, train volume was greatly diminished. Union Station's use had decreased, the depot had fallen into disrepair and the former breathtaking landmark had become an eyesore. It was sold to the city, and the new, smaller depot was built farther north, closer to the rail yards. In 1961, the old building was demolished, nine of the eleven tracks were removed and Fourth Avenue was reopened to car traffic.

ROCK ISLAND DEPOT

The four-story Burlington, Cedar Rapids & Northern (BCR&N) headquarters was built in 1885. Still proudly standing today at 411 First Avenue SE, over 130 years later, it has been best known as the Skogman Building for the past fifty years.

The BCR&N initially linked Burlington and Cedar Rapids and then ran north to St. Paul, Minnesota. As the railway network across the United States expanded and grew, railroad companies merged or bought each other, and names changed. Soon after this building was completed, the BCR&N became a division of the Chicago, Milwaukee & St. Paul line. Before long, it merged with the Chicago, Rock Island & Pacific line, popularly known as the Rock Island Line.

At about the same time as the big Union Station was going up, the Rock Island Line started building a large depot of its own just two blocks away, in the lot between its office building and the Fourth Street tracks. The Milwaukee & Illinois Central depot at 401 First Avenue SE opened for business in 1898, just a year after Union Station. Cedar Rapids now had two fine train depots.

Rock Island and CM&StP Depot stood on what is now Skogman's parking lot. *Courtesy of the History Center, Linn County Historical Society.*

This new passenger station was built of red brick and was 40 by 150 feet with a 50-foot-high tower and a 4-foot clock mounted on the north side of the tower. The lobby and waiting areas were well lit by windows around the upper part of the building. With baggage handlers and porters scrambling to assist, the depot was a hub of activity.

The lifespan of this depot was similar to Union Station—by the late 1950s, it was no longer a viable enterprise and was torn down. Even the office building was too large for the railroad's management and staff, and the building was purchased by the Skogman Homes & Real Estate organization. Skogman installed a neon sign on the top of the building that said, "First Avenue Bldg—Midwest Managed."

During the 1960s, Skogman built a show home on the site of the old depot. The house is long gone, and the depot site has been used as a parking lot for many decades. The four-story Burlington, Cedar Rapids & Northern/ Skogman building was sold in 2018 and remodeled for new tenants.

FOURTH STREET RAIL CORRIDOR

When the leaders of the young city of Cedar Rapids designated Fourth Street as a rail corridor, it resulted in a string of hotels and diners, as well as factories and warehouses, with small depots up and down the tracks. A perfectly straight eighteen-block stretch, from Quaker Oats on the north to Sinclair meatpacking on the south, was quickly developed.

Sidings and spur lines soon branched off to First and Second Streets SE, allowing the efficient movement of goods and suitable development for those business areas.

The following is just a small sampling of downtown businesses that relied on the railroad with their own docks and depots:

Star Wagon: Thirteenth Avenue SE, near the present-day NewBo area
Witwer Wholesale Grocery: First Street SE
Churchill Drug: Second Street SE
Harper & McIntire warehouse: Sixth Avenue SE
Petersen Baking Company: "Home of Peter Pan Bread" on Sixth Avenue SE
Wells Fargo Depot: In the Goodyear/Poore Building on Second Avenue SE

There were also lumber and coal companies on First, Second and Third Streets, as well as warehouses, creameries, furniture manufacturers and paper companies—all with their own railroad spurs and docks.

But not everyone was a fan of the busy tracks, especially motor vehicle drivers who had to sit and wait for trains to pass before they could continue on their way down the various city avenues. In 1933, after a nine-year study, recommendations were presented to the city council to alleviate the "Fourth Street problem." The City Planning Commission recommended elevating the Fourth Street tracks from Twelfth Avenue SE to A Avenue NE. Unfortunately, funds were not available, due to the financial depression of the '30s, and the idea was discarded.

CEDAR RAPIDS & MARION RAILWAY

The horse-drawn streetcar, sometimes called a horsecar or an omnibus, was the earliest form of inner-city public transportation. By the mid-1870s, tracks were laid in Cedar Rapids, and horses pulled the streetcars on steel rails. This type of travel worked well on public streets and roads, due to the low cost, smooth ride and all-weather capability. But the horses were depositing mountains of feces and gallons of urine on the streets every day, and the feeding, grooming and stabling needs were problematic.

A new technology had recently arisen across the country: steam power. Steamboats and steam-powered trains were a success. Steam-powered streetcars were being used in the country's largest cities, including Cedar Rapids. This replaced horse power, but the steam adventure was short-lived.

Before long, a newer technology was introduced: electric streetcars. These new streetcars used a trolley system to travel along rails, drawing electricity from overhead wires.

In the 1880s the city council gave Stephen Dows and Isaac Smith approval to create and operate a system of streetcars, or trolleys, powered by electricity. They installed the lines and power generators, acquired the vehicles and built a trolley barn on Second Street NE.

They improved the existing tracks, and by 1890, there were more than eight miles of trolley tracks in Cedar Rapids, which soon grew to fifteen miles as they expanded the lines to the neighboring town of Kenwood Park just north of the city. Eventually, the lines also reached Marion, following First Avenue/Marion Boulevard.

By 1892, the streetcar system was so finely organized that a trolley would arrive at each stop every fifteen to twenty minutes, which made riding trolleys convenient and efficient. The system allowed people to quickly get to and from their jobs in the city and make easy trips to the store.

The popularity of electric streetcars began its decline in the '30s. City buses were seen as more economical and flexible, as a bus could carry a number of people similar to that in a streetcar but without the tracks, wires and associated infrastructure. In 1938, Cedar Rapids converted all public transportation to buses, and began removing and covering up the rails.

CRANDIC

In 1903, the Cedar Rapids and Iowa City Railway and Light Company was founded by the owners of the Cedar Rapids & Marion Railway. The electric interurban rail line carried the name CRANDIC, an acronym for Cedar Rapids and Iowa City. A building at 328 Second Street SE was converted into a passenger depot, and the construction of twenty-seven miles of railroad beds, bridges and tracks connecting the two cities began immediately.

The electricity needs of this enterprise led to the development of power stations and booster power stations. Eventually, the owners split off Iowa Electric Light & Power Company, which is still in existence today, operating as Alliant Energy.

The first cars carrying passengers made their inaugural trip on August 13, 1904, and the high-speed electric interurban route between the two communities quickly became popular and busy. Cars were in operation from five o'clock in the morning to midnight, with departures every hour. Riders were not only city folks but were also from the small towns and farms and included men, women and children of all ages. Students rode the train to school, and commuters rode the train to work. Passengers headed to doctors' offices and hospitals for medical care. Others went shopping or headed out for dinner or a show. Some were just out to take a train ride through the countryside.

In 1939, six new high-speed cars were added to the fleet. These fast-moving cars experienced a peculiar swaying motion, which led to the promotional jingle "Swing and Sway the CRANDIC Way," but also earned them a derisive nickname, "vomit comets."

CRANDIC provided short line freight service as well, carrying loads such as coal, milk, lumber and grain between the two cities.

In 1945, CRANDIC's passenger service reached its peak, carrying a record 573,307 people that year. Then the decline in ridership began. Usage quickly dropped off, and the interurban was reduced to nine daily runs by 1950. Passenger service was discontinued in 1953, and the CRANDIC became an all-freight rail service.

Today, the local freight line covers sixty miles of track and is still hauling 100,000 carloads a year. Major customers include ADM and Weyerhaeuser, and the CRANDIC freight business continues to expand and grow.

WCF&N

Sixty miles north of Cedar Rapids, Waterloo's streetcar system was growing at the same time. In 1914, the Waterloo, Cedar Falls & Northern (WCF&N) interurban, also known as the Cedar Valley Road, extended service to Cedar Rapids. The Chicago, Rock Island & Pacific line owned the tracks, which ran through Robins, Center Point, Urbana and several other towns. The trip took an hour and fifteen minutes.

The original depot in Cedar Rapids was located at Fourth Avenue and Second Street SE and shared space with the CRANDIC depot for several years.

It eventually needed a new terminal, and in 1937, the WCF&N bought the old Eastman & Bogaard Vet Clinic, nicknamed the Cookie House for its gingerbread-house style. It was located at the northwest corner of A Avenue and Tenth Street NE. A one thousand horsepower generator was installed to boost power for the electric line.

At that point, the WCF&N discontinued its downtown route, and the A Avenue stop was literally the end of the line. Travelers needing to get to downtown Cedar Rapids could either take the bus or a taxi or enjoy a six-block hike.

Interurban service to Waterloo ended in 1956, and the line was shut down. St. Luke's Practical Nursing took over the WCF&N depot building, and then from 1961 to 1973, it was used for St. Luke's student apartments. The building was torn down in 1973 and replaced with a new St. Luke's Diagnostic Center. Today, the entrance to St. Luke's/UnityPoint Emergency Room is in approximately the same spot as the old depot.

16

BRUCEMORE MANSION

And there were houses that breathed. They were filled with memories, with the faded echoes of voices. Drops of tears, drops of blood, the ring of laughter, the edge of tempers that had ebbed and flowed between the walls, into the walls, over the years.
——Nora Roberts

Houses are like people——some you like and some you don't like——and once in a while there is one you love.
——L.M. Montgomery

This book is about the lost buildings and businesses of Cedar Rapids. Brucemore is not lost, but the three powerful families who built it, lived in it, expanded it, cherished it and eventually donated it to the city are gone.

The Brucemore Mansion, located at 2160 Linden Drive SE (originally designated as 1965 First Avenue SE), is a huge redbrick, twenty-one-room Queen Anne mansion situated on a park-like twenty-six-acre estate. The location was once described as "northeast of Cedar Rapids on the Marion Boulevard, out in the country."

For more than a century, the mansion was home to the Sinclair, Douglas and Hall families. These three prominent families—all industrialists, entrepreneurs, philanthropists and city boosters—made Brucemore their home. Their fortunes made and their legacies intact, they graciously left their home to the community that helped build it.

The following is a timeline of events surrounding the development of this fascinating property.

1842: Thomas Sinclair is born in Ireland; the family business was cured hams and bacon.

1862: At age twenty, Thomas Sinclair moves to the United States and starts his own ham and bacon business in New York City.

1871: Thomas marries Caroline Soutter from Philadelphia, and they moved to Cedar Rapids. He is twenty-nine, and she is twenty.

1872: Thomas Sinclair starts a meat packing plant in Cedar Rapids, called TM Sinclair & Co. The business is extremely successful, and the Sinclairs became quite wealthy. Many years later, the plant becomes Wilson & Company and then Farmstead Foods. It finally closes after 120 years in business in 1990.

1881: Thomas Sinclair dies at age thirty-nine when he falls down an elevator shaft at the plant. Caroline Sinclair is widowed at age thirty with six children.

1884: Caroline buys ten acres of land "out in the country," which is barely fifteen blocks away from downtown, and starts building what she names Fairhome.

1886: Caroline completes Fairhome Mansion and lives and raises her kids there for twenty years during the summers. They spend the school year in Philadelphia.

1906: At age fifty-five, kids grown, Caroline trades her mansion for the George and Irene Douglas home in town at 800 Second Avenue SE (later Turner Mortuary, and recently home to the Cedar Rapids History Center). George Douglas had been part owner of Quaker Oats and then started Douglas Starch (later Pennick & Ford).

1907: After swapping homes with Caroline Sinclair, George and Irene Douglas move to the country. George renames the mansion Brucemore, which is a combination of his middle name and the Scottish moors. They buy more land, built a guest cottage and made other improvements, including formal gardens. They have three daughters, the eldest of whom is Margaret.

1923: George Douglas dies at age sixty-five.

1924: Irene Douglas and her daughters continue to live in the mansion. At age twenty-eight, Margaret marries Howard Hall, the owner of Iowa Steel and Iron and Iowa Manufacturing Co. and one of a group that later owned Amana Refrigeration. Margaret and Howard move into the guest

The nineteenth-century Brucemore Mansion was home to the Sinclairs, Douglases and Halls. *Courtesy of Library of Congress.*

cottage behind the mansion and live there for thirteen years. They also have homes in Florida.

1937: Irene Douglas dies. Howard and Margaret move from the cottage to the mansion. They make additional building and property improvements. They have no children, but they own several German shepherds over the years and even keep lions on the property. The MGM lion is related to the Hall lions.

1971: Howard Hall dies at age seventy-seven. Margaret, age seventy-five, keeps living here.

1981: Margaret Hall passes away at age eighty-five. She had bequeathed Brucemore to the city to be operated by the National Trust of Historic Preservation. It is now open to the public for tours and public events.

17

MASONIC LODGES AND SHRINER TEMPLES

What are Masons? Who are the Shriners? Are they the same? Are they different? What is their purpose? Why do they wear those funny red fez hats and drive silly little cars in parades and sponsor circuses? Why are they both so well-respected?
—*The average American*

We build these buildings glorious, if man unbuilded goes, in vain we do the work unless the builder also grows.
—*Edwin Markham*

Freemasonry is the oldest, largest and most widely known fraternity in the world. It dates back hundreds of years to when stonemasons and other craftsmen gathered after work in houses or lodges to encourage and help one another. Over time, Masonry evolved into an organization that accepted members who were not necessarily craftsmen.

Masonry today is a charitable organization dedicated to strengthening a man's character, improving his moral and spiritual outlook and broadening his mental horizons. Masonry seeks to make good men better and emphasizes personal responsibility for one's own conduct. Masons support public education and offer scholarships for continuing education. Equal opportunity of education for all is a basic freedom Masons strenuously support.

Shriners International is a spin-off of Freemasonry. The Shriners organization was built on the principles that guided Freemasonry, while adding an element of fun and philanthropy. Both organizations have distinctive places to meet—Shriners have temples, and Masons generally have lodges. Members of the Masonic lodges can strive to earn a series of Masonic degrees. When a member has completed the third and final degree, he becomes a Master Mason and is then eligible to become a Shriner. So, all Shriners are Masons, but not all Masons are Shriners.

The Shriners' history of contributions to the medical needs of children is humbling. The Shriners Hospitals for Children treat children in need free of charge. Years ago, their contribution to the war on polio was immense and amazingly successful. Today, their focus is on children with burn and spinal cord injuries. Thank you, Shriners.

Cedar Rapids has provided a healthy environment for the growth and services of these related organizations, and over the years, there have been several locations of their temples and lodges.

MASONIC HALL

The original Masonic meeting place was in the grand four-story Union Block building downtown at the northwest corner of First Avenue and Second Street NE. Built in 1862, shops and the Union Bank were on the first floor, offices on the second floor, the Masonic Scottish Rite Temple and social hall were on the third floor and the fourth floor was an auditorium called the Union Opera House. The building was later the Morris Plan headquarters and was replaced in 1970 by the rusted-looking Brenton Bank, now a Wells Fargo bank.

MASONIC TEMPLE

In 1900, a new location was built by the Masons after the removal of the L&L Daniels three-story brick retail store, and it was by far the largest new office building in town. The five-story building sat on the northeast corner of First Avenue and First Street, emblazoned with MASONIC TEMPLE around the parapets.

This impressive structure housed the American Trust & Savings Bank on the ground floor and was the national headquarters of the powerful union, the

Order of Railway Conductors and Brakemen. The building was expensive for the Masons to maintain, and they sold it in 1910 to the ORC&B, resulting in new parapet signage. The building was home to additional businesses, including Haldy's Beauty & Barber, from 1919 to 1959. Haldy's was a wholesale and retail supplier for the beauty and barber industry.

As part of the city's aggressive downtown urban renewal project, in 1969, the building was torn down and was replaced in 1974 by the twenty-five-floor Cedar River Tower apartment building, which stands today.

MASONIC CONSISTORY

High atop the hill at 616 A Avenue NE was a mansion built by Judge George Greene in the late 1800s for his daughter, who had married George Bever. Years later, after the Bevers had passed away, the property was purchased by the Masons, and the mansion served as a temporary temple until the stately Masonic Lodge Hall was built behind it in 1910. Today, the structure still says "MASONIC TEMPLE" on the west-facing façade.

Soon, the lodge was not meeting space needs, and by 1927, the old mansion had been removed, and a large new structure was added. The architect and the general contractor of this addition were the same as the 1910 building, leaving no indication that the entire structure had not been built at one time. Facing A Avenue to the south, the words "SCOTTISH RITE TEMPLE" proudly proclaim its purpose.

Scottish Rite Masons have continued their work there today in the cause of humanity: education, liberty, tolerance and brotherhood.

The Masonic Consistory and Scottish Rite Temple today. *Photo by Peter D. Looney.*

MASONIC LIBRARY

In 1884 the first Masonic library anywhere in the world was opened to the public at 813 First Avenue SE. Until then, books and records had been stored in lodges and homes at various locations around the state. This fine two-story structure was built of stone, with a tall steeple in the front, and it looked like the churches and courthouses being built at the time.

Books kept by Theodore Parvin and Robert Bower of Keokuk had a combined value of $12,000 at the time but were sold to the library at a remarkable price of only $4,000. Acquisitions of books and artifacts continued, and the collections grew so quickly that by 1902, additional neighboring property that held a stately house was acquired and was called the Annex. In 1914, an addition was made to the rear of the main building. Yet by 1953, the facility proved too small and crowded. All of the buildings were demolished, and a new grand facility opened on the same site in 1955.

This large, white marble structure houses the library collection in four floors of book stacks, as well as several museums, special exhibits, conference rooms, vaults, and the administrative offices of the Grand Lodge of Iowa AF&AM.

Today, the Iowa Masonic Library is regarded as one of the best facilities in the world for performing Masonic research. As stated on its website, "The Library houses over 150,000 volumes of which thousands are rare Masonic books for the serious researcher, and a circulating collection for the casual reader. The Library also collects materials dealing with non-Masonic topics. The Iowa collection contains materials dealing with Iowa history, government, education, social history, religion, etc. In addition, the Library boasts a number of volumes on spirituality, religion, philosophy, history, literature, and biography."

SHRINER TEMPLE

The enormous redbrick El Kahir Shriner Temple was built in 1927 on the hill at 520 A Avenue NE, just west of the Scottish Rite Temple. An impressive landmark, the building was of Moorish-style design, with four huge, unforgettable white-domed corners.

The auditorium had a seating capacity of over two thousand, and the facility was home to a variety of Shriner and entertainment events. But when the Great Depression hit, the Shriners quickly discovered that the cost to maintain the structure was excessive, and they sought out renters to share the space and help defray costs. In 1932, they contracted with the Cedar Rapids Board of Education to rent the auditorium for all high school physical education classes and indoor athletic events, as well as various school assemblies. But by the late 1930s, the Shriners had to find a more affordable location.

In 1940, the main floor was rented out for skating, and the Temple Roller Rink opened. It was immediately popular, and roller-skating lasted there for over thirteen years.

Meanwhile, the Iowa National Guard had taken up residence in the temple in 1941. It shared the facility not only with the roller rink, but with Collins Radio Company, which used its space for an assembly plant during World War II. In 1951, the National Guard bought the building, and it became known as the Shrine Armory. Part of the auditorium was sectioned off into classrooms for the Guard. Recruitment activities were held there as well.

In 1953, the skating rink closed, and in the following decade, the guard moved out. By 1967, the entire building had been vacated, and was torn down in 1968 in preparation for the building of Interstate 380.

The El Kahir Shrine Temple, later known as the Shrine Armory, home to the Temple Roller Rink and the National Guard. *Courtesy of the History Center, Linn County Historical Society.*

SHRINE OFFICE AND EMBASSY CLUB

By 1939, the Shriners had downsized and moved their offices into the Montrose Hotel building at 223 Third Avenue SE. They opened their Embassy Club, which was a popular place to dine and socialize. By 1946, the Shriners had found a better location for the club and offices and moved out of the Montrose.

SHRINER EMBASSY CLUB

In 1947, the El Kahir Shriners purchased and moved into the Palmer Building at 125 Fifth Street SE. This was an excellent location, and they remained there for forty years.

The Fifth Street location served their needs well, housing the Shrine business offices, the Shrine Circus office and the Embassy Club and Dining Room. The third floor offered an auditorium, dance floor and lounge, while the street level was rented to retail and other businesses. The Shrine organization was continuing to experience growth, and by 1978, there were more than 1,600 El Kahir Shrine members in the Cedar Rapids area.

EL KAHIR SHRINE TEMPLE

A new location better suited to their needs was found. It included storage space for their parade floats and mini vehicles. In 1988, they relocated to the large corner property at 1400 Blairs Ferry Road and Council Street NE, which had formerly housed the United State Bank drive-up facility. And twenty-seven years later, they were ready to move again. After the Shriners left, the University of Iowa Community Credit Union (now called GreenState Credit Union) bought the property, removed the old buildings, and built a new structure in 2017.

EL KAHIR SHRINE

In 2015, the Shriners bought a corner lot in the rapidly growing business park in Hiawatha at 905 Tower Terrace and Stamy Road. They built a new, permanent facility. They continue to play a key philanthropic role in the Cedar Rapids community. Again, thank you, Shriners.

18

ALL-IOWA FAIR

It seems people can find almost any excuse to throw a party. And a party is even more fun when the whole community is invited. That's the principle behind fairs.
—Bill Thornbrook, Journal of Antiques and Collectibles

If you ever start feeling like you have the goofiest, craziest, most dysfunctional family in the world, all you have to do is go to a local fair. Because five minutes at the fair, you'll be going, "you know, we're alright. We are dang near royalty."
—Jeff Foxworthy

How many people do you know who have thrown up on the Scrambler or a Tilt-A-Whirl or another carnival ride? "A lot of people," is the answer.
—Mike Birbiglia

Cedar Rapids boasts a long history of fairs. Fairs provide entertainment, fun and educational opportunities that can linger for the rest of the year. And the excitement of going to the fairgrounds with your friends and family is such a unique experience.

They often present big-name concerts, but Iowa fairs also have individual flavors that seem to reflect our rural interests. Watch rodeos and races, take the kids to the petting zoos, wander the stalls of the livestock barns, visit all of the exhibition halls, check out the blue-ribbon winners for food and flowers and livestock and don't miss the butter sculpture.

Be sure to check out the Midway—try your hand at the games and win some cheap prizes and a giant stuffed bear. Go on the carnival rides, get on the Tilt-A-Whirl, go through the funhouse and maybe even visit a few sideshows.

Hungry? If not, stay home because you will find snow cones and cotton candy and popcorn and dogs on a stick and giant turkey legs and taffy. You can get every kind of fried food imaginable. You can get fried food that was previously unimaginable. And it is all amazingly wonderful.

Iowans were fiercely proud of their fairs back in the day. Fairs were held everywhere. There used to be several fairgrounds in Cedar Rapids and the surrounding areas, but the big one was the All-Iowa Fair.

ACHIEVEMENT DAY/ALL-IOWA FAIR/HAWKEYE DOWNS FAIR

Dairy cattle shows in Cedar Rapids and Des Moines led to what eventually became the largest and most popular fair in eastern Iowa. The Linn County 4-H club was founded in 1924. The Farm Bureau had been sponsoring two dairy calf clubs: a Guernsey and a Holstein Heifer club. The members of these 4-H calf clubs had been showing their calves at the Marion Interstate Fair and at the Waterloo Cattle Congress. The Linn County Farm Bureau was also sponsoring appreciation events, which were held in mid-August.

Achievement Day was an opportunity for club members to show their livestock as well as projects they had worked on throughout the year, with exhibits, demonstrations and revues. After searching for an appropriate Cedar Rapids location for their shows and appreciation events, Farm Bureau and 4-H quickly realized that the new Frontier Amusement Park was an obvious fit. Frontier Park's racetrack, rodeo grounds and huge grandstand had been built south of town on Sixth Street SW just a couple of years earlier. So, in 1927, 4-H Achievement Day found its new location.

Meanwhile, another annual mid-August farm-related event was looking for a new venue. The All-Iowa Jersey Cattle Show wanted to relocate from Des Moines to Cedar Rapids and, in 1935, settled at Frontier Park. The next year, the group changed the name of the event and broadened its scope.

The first All-Iowa Fair was held in 1936. The next year, the park's name was changed to Hawkeye Downs, and year after year, the All-Iowa Fair continued to grow as the races, exhibits, livestock judging and midway rides all continued to increase in popularity.

Ownership of the property changed hands several times, and in 1949, the city handed over the deed for the property's entire seventy acres to the All-Iowa Fair Association. The fair's success continued, but in the 1960s, the Linn County 4-H parted ways, and its annual fair moved to the fairgrounds in Central City.

The All-Iowa Fair remained popular for several decades but eventually began experiencing declining attendance. In 2000, the Fair Association made two major changes: it was renamed the Hawkeye Downs Fair and the date of the fair was moved to early June.

"The old name had too many bad vibes," said Jim Amstutz, the fair's general manager. "The event had sunk in stature significantly. But everyone knows what Hawkeye Downs is, because of the speedway. Changing the date to being one of the first fairs in the state, instead of one of the last, seemed to work. We did better, there was substantial improvement."

But apparently not enough improvement, and after the poorly attended 2006 event, the fair was discontinued permanently.

Other fairgrounds in the area include:

Linn County Fair: Marion, Scott's Prairie, southeast of downtown (1864–70)

Fairgrounds: North of Coe College (1870)

Fairgrounds: Between Cedar Rapids and Marion (1871–77)

Driving Park: Between Second and Third Avenues at Fourteenth Street SE (1890–95)

Driving Park: Between F and G Avenues and Thirteenth Street NW (1896–1907)

Marion Interstate Fair Park: 2401 Indian Creek Road (1901–26)

Cedar Rapids Carnival Grounds: Twenty-Ninth Street and B Avenue NE (1930–34)

Linn County Fairgrounds: Central City (1937–present); Wapsi Valley Fairgrounds (1888–1936)

19

YMCAs AND YWCAs

I can be changed by what happens to me. But I refuse to be reduced by it.
—Maya Angelou

Start where you are. Use what you have. Do what you can.
—YMCA, Holyoke, Massachusetts

I love the Y for a myriad of reasons. One, during months when I don't work out much, I know my membership dues help support critical community programs. Two, there's a great cross section of folks who use the Y, and I usually get to chat with people outside my own demographic. Three, the Y is unpretentious. I never feel like anyone is judging me. Walking in wearing welding clothes and carrying a swimsuit in a plastic grocery bag? That's cool. I'd never try that at the fancy clubs.
—Cara Briggs Farmer, Cedar Rapids

The YMCAs and YWCAs across our great country have a clear purpose: to promote community wellness and family enrichment through programs that focus on youth development, healthy living and social responsibility. The Y makes accessible the support and opportunities that empower people and communities. The Y nurtures the potential of every youth, teen and adult; improves the nation's health and well-being; and provides opportunities to give back and support neighbors.

The Young Men's Christian Association was founded in London, England, on June 6, 1844, in response to unhealthy social conditions arising in the big cities during the Industrial Revolution. The centralization of industry had brought many rural young men needing jobs into the cities. They worked ten to twelve hours a day, six days a week. Far from home and family, these young men often lived at the workplace. They slept crowded into rooms over the company's shop—a location thought to be safer than London's tenements and streets. Outside the shop were open sewers, pickpockets, thugs, beggars, drunks and abandoned children running wild.

A group of businessmen organized that first YMCA to substitute Bible study and prayer for life on the streets. They provided lists of Christian boardinghouses, libraries and meeting halls, most of them in rented quarters. The YMCA idea was unusual because it crossed the rigid lines that separated different churches and social classes. This openness was a trait that would eventually lead the YMCA to include all men, women and children, regardless of race, religion or nationality. Its target of meeting social needs in the community was clear from the start.

By 1851, the Y had arrived in the United States, and in 1868, the it started offering its programs in Cedar Rapids.

It wasn't until the 1880s that YMCAs began putting up buildings with gyms and swimming pools, along with auditoriums and reading rooms. Hotel-like bedrooms were designed in every new YMCA building, although that feature ended in the 1960s.

In Cedar Rapids, after twenty years of temporary rented locations, a dedicated YMCA building was built in 1888 at the intersection of First Avenue and First Street NE, backing up to the river. The 1890 Cedar Rapids City Directory stated:

> *The Young Men's Christian Association—this organization is for the benefiting of men in four ways: socially, physically, mentally and spiritually. The Association has erected one of the finest buildings in the city. It has a fine gymnasium, a nicely arranged bath room, and one of the largest swimming baths in the country connected with an association. On the second floor is a well-appointed reading room and a large library. Cedar Rapids has the honor of erecting the first YMCA building in the state and one of the first in the northwest for its young men.*

The marble swimming pool was beautiful, but the water temperature was notoriously frigid due to its source—the Cedar River flowing past its back door.

Later, this building went on to house the offices of the Cedar Rapids Waterworks, McDougall & McDowell Furniture, Central Iowa Paper Co.

& Job Printing, the original Turner Funeral Home, a multitude of union offices, Standard Appliance and a Jack's Store. Drive by there today, and you'll see the tall Tree of Five Seasons aluminum sculpture that has been standing proudly in a small pedestrian plaza since 1996.

In 1918, the YMCA moved out and into a new building farther up First Avenue at the intersection with Fifth Street NE. This stately five-story brick building included a new pool, a gymnasium, a small theater and a ninety-room dormitory. For several years, a youth Keen Teen Club occupied a lower corner of the building, and later, Emil's Deli had a location there. A large annex was added in 1973, and the façade was remodeled and updated in 1980.

The YMCA relocated to a new facility at 207 Seventh Avenue SE in 2002, where it remains today. The big First Avenue building was demolished, and a Cedar Rapids Bank & Trust building stands there now. In 2018, the YMCA of the Metro Cedar Rapids Area celebrated its 150th year.

YWCA

The YWCA grew out of the Bohemian Young Women's Union, which was founded in 1891. It officially organized as the Young Women's Christian Association in 1893 and occupied upper levels of various downtown buildings. The organization's goals were to improve lives and empower local women. In 1898, it opened a cafeteria, and by 1904, it was renting a large space at 110 Third Street SE, next door to what eventually became the Iowa Theater, now Theatre Cedar Rapids.

Following a successful fund drive that raised $80,000, the vacant St. Paul's Methodist Church and parsonage at 318 Fifth Street SE were acquired in 1911. The YWCA thrived at this location, offering temporary lodging, fitness programs, swimming classes, meals, lectures, reading and discussions for women.

The oldest structures were removed, and additions were built in the 1950s. Clubs were formed, including the Twenty Forty Club for women and the Y Teens Club for youth.

Over the years, the YWCA continued to meet the needs critical to women's lives through exercise classes to increase physical stamina, support for businesswomen and, eventually, shelter and support for those experiencing domestic violence.

The old YWCA building at 318 Fifth Street SE as it looks in 2020. *Photo by Peter D. Looney.*

As women's needs evolved, focus was clarified for the Cedar Rapids area's need for critical support services, and it grew distinct from the YWCA organization's mission, leading to the name change of "Waypoint" in 2001.

The word "waypoint" is defined as a resting spot on a journey. By providing individuals with the tools and support they need to rebuild their lives, Waypoint is giving them the opportunity to make the necessary moves to attain stability. Waypoint's tradition of assisting women and children in Cedar Rapids and surrounding Iowa communities persists as it continues to find new ways to help individuals in crisis.

20

SUNSHINE MISSION

Charity and love are the same—with charity you give love, so don't just give money but reach out your hand instead.
—Mother Teresa

One of the most important things you can do on this earth is to let people know they are not alone.
—Shannon L. Alder

If you're not making someone else's life better, then you're wasting your time. Your life will become better by making other lives better.
—Will Smith

The Sunshine Mission was active in Cedar Rapids for seventy-two years, starting in 1895 and operating until 1967. It was a nondenominational Christian ministry that was supported by many local churches and created and overseen by a mission board. Sermons were offered, the gospel was shared, poor children were fed, needy families were assisted, homeless men were given a place to shower and sleep, and women were given assistance and training. Day care for working mothers was offered so that boys, girls and babies had a place that was safe.

Francis "Daddy" Ward (1854–1933) was the founding pastor and superintendent from 1895 to 1912. Then his son, Frank H. Ward (1879–

1961), took over from 1912 until his retirement in 1952, followed by Reverend Walter Pierce from 1952 to 1958, and finally, Henry Mensinger relocated from Chicago to preside from 1959 until the closing of the mission in 1967.

The Mission operated out of seven locations over the years:

1. 225 First Street SE: This original location was simply four upstairs rooms in a rooming house (1895–96).
2. 109 First Street NE: Next door to the YMCA, operating out of storage rooms in the Arcade Hotel, which was later known as the Gorman Hotel (1896–1900).
3. 303 Sixth Avenue SE: In the old Second United Presbyterian church, which in later years was home to Metropolitan Supply Company (1901–12).
4. 221 First Street SE: A second location (1904–05).
5. 116 First Avenue NE: Another branch location opened here (1906–07).
6. 101 First Street SE, second entrance at 95 First Avenue SE: The big corner building (1912–29).
7. 121 Second Street NE: When this building was removed during the downtown urban renewal project (along with its neighbor, the old Greene's Opera House building), the mission ceased operations (1930–67).

The Sunshine Mission's sixth location, at 101 First Street SE, was unique for a couple of reasons. The building started in 1870 as the two-story Adams Building, with Adams Drugs as the original tenant. Later, the Rudolf Grocery Company used the location for a warehouse. Then, a third story was added, with a huge sign on top proclaiming, "Jesus, The Light of the World." The Sunshine Mission remodeled the space and arranged it with offices and a chapel on the first floor; home for girls and a nursery on the second floor; meeting rooms, prayer rooms and spaces

Francis "Daddy" Ward (*center*) posing with helpers in front of the Sixth Avenue location of the Sunshine Mission in the early 1900s. *Author's collection.*

for businesswomen on the third floor; and lodging and showers for men in the basement.

The back of the building was used by the John B. Turner Funeral Home from 1900 until 1916, after the mortuary left the old YMCA building across the street. Sunshine Mission moved to its final location on Second Street NE when the federal government acquired the First Street property for a new riverfront courthouse and post office.

PART IV

───────── ✳ ─────────

HOTELS

Arriving guests signed the registry and paid their money. A room without a mattress rented for one dollar; a mattress for two people cost an extra twenty-five cents, and blankets, sheets, and pillows another fifty cents. Each guest was given a bucket of water from an outside hydrant, along with a scuttle of firewood in the winter.
—The Motel in America

The great advantage of a hotel is that it is a refuge from home life.
—*George Bernard Shaw*

Room service is nice. Ooh-la-la, a hotel! At home, it's laundry and school lunches.
—*Dolores O'Riordan,* The Cranberries

What is the difference between a motel and a hotel? Motels are a place to sleep. They are designed to accommodate traveling motorists with parking for your vehicle close to your room's door. Back in the day, the good motel chains were Howard Johnson, Holiday Inn, Travelodge, Quality Inn and Best Western. Now, there are the budget motels—Econolodge, Rodeway, Red Roof, Super 8 and Motel 6.

Most of these motels offer continental help-yourself breakfasts. In addition, the single-owner, mom-and-pop roadside motels that used to dominate the roadways can still be found off the beaten paths today.

Now, of course, there are a lot of nicer motels, ones that offer more and more amenities, like swimming pools, saunas, workout rooms and even suites—places like Ramada Inn, Hampton Inn, Heartland, Fairfield,

Comfort, LaQuinta, Hometown, Residence, Country Inn, Days Inn, Baymont, Americinn, Mainstay and many others.

But hotels are quite different—they are more than a place to sleep. Hotels are destinations. They offer dining, dancing, drinking, gift shops, spas and banquet and meeting facilities. And as Delores O'Riordan pointed out, room service.

Hotels are situated in downtown areas, business districts and near busy interstate intersections. They are often near airports, casinos, sports arenas and other destination spots. They are a place to stay and, not so long ago, maybe even a place to live.

Cedar Rapids has the Roosevelt. Built in 1927 on First Avenue, it was once a glamorous hotel with all of the amenities of the day. The a twelve-story masterpiece is still a fine structure and an important part of our downtown. Its focus now is rental units instead of lodging for travelers.

But the other old grand downtown hotels? They're all gone—long gone.

We've recently lost another wonderful destination, Cooper's Mill Hotel, originally built in 1972 as the Village Inn Hotel but now a victim of the mighty Cedar River overflowing its banks more than once in the last decade. Cooper's Mill's valuables were auctioned off, and its structure was dismantled in 2017.

There are still some nice hotels in Cedar Rapids, though. The Doubletree by Hilton, situated downtown and connected to the US Cellular Center, is the complex previously known as the Five Seasons Center. On Collins Road, the Marriott Hotel was formerly Collins Plaza. The Ramada by Wyndham on Thirty-Third Avenue in southwest Cedar Rapids was called Fairbridge for a while. Before that, it was the Clarion, but forever in our hearts, it is the Sheraton—built, owned and lovingly operated by the Zazza family.

KIRKWOOD HOTEL

There is a new hotel in town. It's called the Hotel at Kirkwood Center. It is Cedar Rapids' only AAA rated, four diamond hotel, and it has seventy-one sleeping rooms, the Class Act Restaurant, a ballroom, an amphitheater and state-of-the-art conference facilities. Located on the south end of the Kirkwood College campus, it's a boutique hotel that offers everything a traveler desires. And because the Hotel is also a teaching facility, the professional staff is required to bring service at the highest level. Built as a learning laboratory, students serve in many support roles to prepare them to enter the professional hospitality industry. The four-story inn opened in 2010 and is a stylish and sophisticated hotel with modern flair, offering an impressive array of services, including bell staff and valet parking.

THE LONGBRANCH

What began as a Western-themed restaurant has evolved into a favorite venue for lodging, socializing, dining, parties, receptions, meetings, reunions, conventions and other special events.

In 1968, the DeLong family opened the Longbranch just off First Avenue NE, on Twixt Town Road. The family did most of the designing and construction on the original restaurant. The four sons provided the manual labor after school and on weekends, scraping and painting old wagon wheels, pouring concrete and laying block. Family artistic talents were included as well, and Old West–themed murals are found throughout the original buildings.

The restaurant featured the choicest cuts, the most delicious sides and decadent desserts that highlighted Iowa flavors. Many of the original recipes came from family members, friends and employees. Business was brisk at this popular restaurant, with guests having to wait, on many nights, up to three hours for a seat.

In 1970, an additional dining room was constructed, doubling the original seating for dining. A large convention hall was opened behind the original restaurant in 1974, featuring a motorized stage for dinner theater performances starring the Old Barn Players.

In 1978, the Longbranch constructed a four-story, fifty-four-unit motel, plus the Skyliner, a revolving bar on the fourth floor. A popular nightclub called Kitty's Rock Showplace opened on the main restaurant's floor and featured live music.

Another four-story hotel addition, including a full-service health club, indoor heated pool, whirlpool, dry sauna and large garden-like atrium area with billiards, games and a café opened in 1985. The Longbranch now had two restaurants, a café, a bar, convention areas and 106 rooms for rent.

Today, karaoke and trivia nights pack the house, and for the past twenty years or so, the Longbranch has also hosted all-you-can-eat Thursday Night Wing Night, which is wildly popular.

"We usually get 200 to 300 people every Thursday night who come out to enjoy our wings," said second-generation owner Doug DeLong. The signature hot wings are served New York style, with homemade blue cheese and ranch dressing, celery and carrots.

"We have a lot of regulars who come back week after week, and year after year, that just love the Longbranch," said DeLong. "The restaurant has been here for over 50 years now, so the locals know us as being a very good restaurant, and just a fun place."

DOWNTOWN HOTELS

Over the years, almost all of the hotels in Cedar Rapids were downtown on the east side. But there was one particular hotel on the west side of the river that was there for almost ninety years. The Kingston Hotel at 110 First Street NW was built in 1880, became the Windsor Hotel from 1900 to 1968 and was torn down around 1970. During its run, it had two popular lounges: the Twilite Room, featuring live music, and the Office Restaurant & Lounge. Both were active during the 1960s. The entire area eventually became a busy Vicker's gas station.

The rest of the downtown hotels were on the east side of the river.

Built in 1905, the Cedar Rapids Hotel, a seven-story state-of-the-art hotel was located at 233 Third Avenue SE. It was created and funded by the Cedar Rapids Commercial Club, a forerunner of the chamber of commerce. It then officially reopened as the Montrose Hotel in 1906. The Montrose housed the Shriners' Embassy Club from 1939 to 1946, the popular Java Room from 1940 to 1956 and the popular Hurdle & Halter lounge from 1940 to 1948. The Montrose closed in 1981, sat empty, and was torn down in 1988. The Town Centre office building replaced it in 1992.

The five-story Magnus Hotel was built in 1912 right next to the tracks at 324 Second Avenue SE. It backed up to the Allison and provided lodging to travelers and locals until 1978. The lounge in the Magnus had several interesting names over the years, including Magnus Tap Room (1975), Golden Guitar Lounge (1974), Three Twenty-Four Room (1971–72), Stables Lounge (1968–70), Pink Garter (1964), Silver Leaf Room (1946) and Stables (1940).

The building came down in 1983 and was replaced with a parking ramp.

The Allison

As the young pioneer city of Cedar Rapids grew, more and more hotels were in demand. The premier location for a hotel was at 325 First Avenue SE, next to the Fourth Street tracks. This is where the elegant three-story Northwestern Hotel was built in 1875.

By 1885, the Northwestern had been renamed the Clifton Hotel. But in February 1903, the Clifton tragically caught fire and burned quickly. Eleven guests trapped inside were unable to get out.

With the building destroyed, the property was cleared, and a new, five-story hotel was built and advertised as "the first completely fireproof building in the city." The new facility opened in 1905 and was called the Allison Hotel, named for the respected, long-serving Iowa senator William Allison.

The new hotel catered to traveling businessmen and featured a superb restaurant. It was home to the Allison Pool Hall, which had a separate entrance around the corner, on the tracks side. The building also provided the space for the popular Bishops Cafeteria, which opened in 1922.

The Allison was located directly across the Fourth Street tracks from one train depot and just a block away from an even bigger depot, and for eighty years, the building was vital and busy. But as buildings age, so does the clientele, and the quality and upkeep grow harder to maintain. The business became less of a popular destination and more of a temporary home to low-income residents. The deteriorating building finally became a target for urban renewal.

Bishop's Cafeteria closed in January 1981, and the Allison closed for good two years later. In 1983, along with the Magnus, the Allison Hotel building was demolished. The grounds were filled in and black-topped with asphalt, and the properties served as parking lots for over thirty years. Finally, in 2016, a four-story parking ramp was built there for the convenience of downtown workers, shoppers and visitors to US Cellular Center events.

Blocks

In the late 1800s and into the early 1900s, when a large downtown multi-floor office building happened to be built on a corner lot, the structure was generally designated with the title of "block." Examples include Union Block at the northwest corner of First Avenue and Second Street, which eventually became the Morris Plan; Jim Block at the southwest corner of A

Avenue and Third Street, which became part of the Majestic Theater; and the Kimball Block at the northwest corner of Second Avenue and Third Street, eventually the location of the MNB building.

These downtown buildings were built by prominent families, and all of the corner buildings had the names of the family name followed by "Block" inscribed on the parapets. If a family was wealthy enough to erect several corner buildings, they would inscribe the identical name. For instance, at the intersection of First Avenue and Third Street, there were Waterhouse Block buildings on three of the corners: Boyson Drug/Iowa Theater on the southeast corner, Taft Dry Goods/Kresge's Five-and-dime on the southwest corner and the Grand Hotel on the northeast corner—all inscribed with "Waterhouse."

The northeast corner Waterhouse Block, at 300 First Avenue NE, was built in 1877 and was originally three stories. It became the Grand Hotel in 1880, and a fourth story was added. The Grand was the city's finest hotel of its time and catered to elite travelers, popular lecturers and international performers bringing their shows to town.

In 1906, a theater was added, called the Bijou Theater and renamed the Lyric Theater in 1907. In 1920, it became the Grand Theater and stayed in use until the early 1930s. The Grand Hotel closed in 1947, and the entire building was torn down in the 1950s.

Interesting Hotels

The smaller downtown hotels that came and went over the years are really interesting. These places, particularly the ones from the earlier years, are long gone and mostly forgotten, and it is OK to say, "I did not know that there was a hotel there!"

They include:

Hi-Way Hotel: 113 A Avenue NE (1937–46)

Palace Hotel: 219½ First Street SE (1925–34); **Plaza Hotel** (1935–60)

The Cedar Hotel: 106 Third Avenue SE (1925–35); **Milner Hotel** (1936–58); **Marley Hotel** (1960–68)

Leone Hotel: 111 First Avenue SE (1917–20); **Moore Hotel** (1922–28)

Central Hotel: 211 Fourth Avenue SE (1917–45)

Lincoln Hotel: Along the tracks in the former Perfection Manufacturing building at 403 Second Avenue SE (1915–40); **Taft Hotel**: which also provided space to the original Hall Bicycle store location (1940–75)

Marshall Hotel: 103 Third Avenue SE (1914–19); **Victoria Hotel** (1920–68)

Fabyan Hotel: 514 Second Avenue SE (1913–29)

Hotel Hoagland: 315 Second Avenue SE (1912–14); **Isis Hotel** (1916–28)

Helmer Hotel: 215 First Street SE (1910–28); **Rex Hotel** (1929)

Astoria House: 416 C Avenue NE (1909–10)

Russell House: 119 Fourth Street SE, along the tracks (1903–10)

Parlor City Hotel: 207 Fourth Avenue SE (1902–11); **Fourth Avenue Hotel** (1912–16)

Stein's Hotel: 306 First Street SE (1890–95); **Farmer's Hotel** (1898)

Schaffer House: 117 Third Street NE, later the site of the Jim Block in 1920 (1890–1900)

Union Hotel: In the Weller & Dows building at 219 Third Street SE (1890–1906); **Hutchinson Hotel** (1909–12); **Royal Hotel** (1913–46)

Park House: 72 First Street SE (1890–93)

New Empire House: 31 Third Avenue SE (1888–98)

Palace Hotel: 316 First Avenue NE, featuring "The Palace Sample Room—Wines, Liquor, Cigars" (1886–1901); **Delavan Hotel**: "Cedar Rapids' Premier Hotel, $2.50 per day" (1902–43); **Norva Hotel**: "with the Purple Cow Nite Club" (1944–66); **Five Seasons/Doubletree by Hilton** (1979–present)

Pullman Hotel: 320 First Avenue NE, located next door the previous hotels (1885–1967)

National Hotel: 319 First Avenue SE, across the street from the previous hotel (1885–1905); **College Inn** (1907–17); **Eleanor Hotel** (1918–39)

Stark's Hotel: 201 First Street SE (1885–1922)

Stark's Hotel: 97 Second Avenue SE (1914–29); **Riverview Hotel** (1937–46)

New York House: 322 Third Street SE (1884–1903)

Ahwaga Hotel: 50 Second Avenue SE (1883–84); **Hotel Denison** (1885–86); **Globe Hotel** (1888–92)

Globe Hotel: 218 Second Avenue SE (1885–1937)

Chandler House: 72 Third Street NE, later became the location of the Danceland building in 1926 (1883–85); **Williams House** (1886–88); **Ralston House** (1890–95)

Lawrence House: 70 B Avenue NE (1880–98)

Jefferson House: 110 Fourth Street NE (1876–83)

Chicago House: 84 A Avenue NE (1875–95)

Central House: Third Avenue and Second Street SE (1875–84); **New York House** (1885–1903)

Brown's Hotel: 107 First Street NE (1872–80); **Southern Hotel** (1882–90); **Arcade Hotel** (1890–1901); **European Hotel** (1903–04); **Gorman's European** (1904–12); **Gorman Hotel** (1913–18); **Riverside Inn** (1919–36)

Cedar Rapids House: 201 A Avenue NE (1870–1919)

Centennial Hotel: 82 First Avenue SE (1870–80); **Pullman House** (1882–93)

Depot Hotel & Dining: 326 First Avenue NE, eventually became part of the Five Seasons/Doubletree by Hilton (1870–80)

Valley City House: First Avenue and Third Street SE (1869–83)

Empire House Hotel: 201 Third Avenue SE, "Free omnibus and baggage wagon to & from every train. Stages leave this house daily for Iowa City" (1854–70); **Park Avenue Hotel** (1870–76); **Cedar Rapids City Hall** (1876–1910)

American House Hotel: Second Avenue and Second Street SE; "Boarding by the day or week, and offering to the public a first class restaurant & saloon known as the 'Old England.' Stock ale and porter in bottles and in kegs. Our tables are supplied with the most substantial edibles" (1860s); moved to First Street and Second Avenue SE (1870–73)

Dubuque House: 410 C Avenue NE, where the first Catholic Mass in Linn County was celebrated in 1853 by Father Hannon, who traveled 30 miles by stagecoach from Iowa City (1850–1911)

The Coffman House: On Second Street SE, sleeping quarters and social hall (1850s)

The Astor House: First Street and Fourth Avenue SE (1848)

The Ganning-Dwyer Hotel: Third Avenue and Third Street SE, the city's first purpose-built hotel, later the location of Armstrongs (1847)

But the first place to provide lodging for travelers was Osgood Shepherd's log cabin home and tavern and inn, in the late 1830s. It was along the river near the intersection of First Avenue and First Street NE long before streets were platted.

PART V

—— ✐ ——

DEPARTMENT STORES

When you think about it, department stores are kind of like museums.
—Andy Warhol

You walk into a retail store, whatever it is, and if there's a sense of entertainment
and excitement and electricity, you wanna be there.
—Howard Schultz

I'm not from a retail background, but I am a shopper.
—Edward Lampert

S ome of our local history lovers' best memories are from when they
visited the downtown department stores. Maybe they were kids, and
they were awed by the lights and the displays at Christmastime. Or
their parents had given them a nickel and a few pennies and turned them
loose in the five-and-dime. Or maybe they stared in wonder at the row after
row of chairs, sofas and beds. Or maybe it was time to shop for back-to-
school clothing, and they were excited about all of the styles and selections.
And when they were tired or hungry, they climbed up on a stool at a tearoom
or luncheon counter.

Downtown was not only *the* place where you'd find these incredible
stores, it was the *only* place. It wasn't until the 1950s that they started
moving out to the suburban shopping centers, plazas and malls—Town &

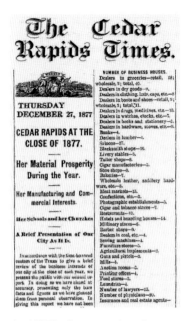

An 1877 business overview. *Courtesy of the* Cedar Rapids Times.

Country, Lindale and Westdale. These are great places, and the idea makes perfect sense, but it sadly brought a change to the downtown, and everyone misses the grand old stores.

And even relocating to the malls doesn't ensure the viability or perpetual success of a store. Today, the big-name stores are pretty much gone. They're all becoming memories. Gordmans closed in 2020. In 2018, Younkers and Sears closed. We'd already lost Kmart just a few years before and Montgomery Wards a decade before that. And the Shopkos and Spartans and Giant Stores and Jack's Discounts are long gone. Who's still left in town? Target, Walmart, Kohls, Von Maur, and Slumberland, and there are still a lot of smaller specialized shops around town.

I guess instead of worrying about the present, we can take a look at the past. Let's start way back, when Cedar Rapids was still a young city. We'll look at some of the original hardware and dry goods stores, furniture stores, department stores, five-and-dimes and clothing stores. These are the places where people would go to shop.

OLD STORES

1844: Joseph and George Greene open the first retail store in Rapids City, Iowa, five years before the name change to Cedar Rapids.

1846: L&L Daniels dry goods is opened by Lowell and Lawson Daniels after four years in Marion with their brothers, Preston and Addison. They build a nice three-story brick building at First and First. It is removed in 1900 for the construction of the Masonic Temple/ORC&B Building, now the site of Cedar River Tower Apartments.

1854: Sampson Bever comes to town, accumulating over four thousand acres of nearby land east of town, and runs a general store prior to his banking endeavors that begin in 1858.

1855: J.S. Cook runs a retail store—dry goods and groceries—at 424 First Avenue NE. By 1874, he has shifted his energies to the wholesale business, eventually calling it the Welch-Cook-Beals Company. The retail store carries on with a new partner into the 1880s. The First Avenue site later becomes the Elks Lodge and later yet the Chamber of Commerce.

1870: Larimer Hardware takes up residence at 120 First Street SE, "having purchased the stock of TM Jones, successor to E Berresford. One of the largest stores in the city! Iron, nails, horseshoes, shelf hardware." Larimer remains in business until 1900.

1870: Isham Dry Goods opens at 308 First Avenue NE before selling to Clark & Barton Dry Goods, which continues operating from 1876 to 1880.

1884: Kubias Hardware opens. Frank Kubias is a Czech immigrant who grew up on a farm in rural Linn County, moved to town, and opened the hardware store at 206 First Street SE with a partner. By 1888, he is the sole owner. During the downtown revitalization of the late 1960s, every old building in the first two blocks of First Street is demolished. Kubias Hardware had moved to 311 Third Street SE, and finally, after three generations of family ownership and 102 years of operations, Kubias closes in 1986.

FURNITURE STORES

In 1888, Russian immigrant Henry Smulekoff came to America, arriving in Linn County a year later, peddling dry goods in the rural areas. He saved every penny he could, and in 1890, he opened Smulekoff's Dry Goods Store after purchasing an existing one-room shop on May's Island. Within four years, he had shifted his focus to furniture, built a larger store adjacent to the original and named it Smulekoff's Island Store. The Island Store experienced great success, but with the city intending on taking over the island for government purposes, Mr. Smulekoff sold the building in 1910 and moved his business to the west side of the river. His business thrived at 111 Third Avenue SW. In 1929, Mr. Smulekoff retired to California and died the next year at the age of sixty-nine. Store management was carried on by Henry's sons. Needing more space in 1942, Smulekoff's moved across the river to its final location, a landmark six-story building at the corner of First Street and Third Avenue SE, eventually growing to be the largest furniture store in Iowa. The business ran its course, and in 2014, Smulekoff's ceased operations.

An ad in the August 11, 1946 Cedar Rapids *Gazette* promoting the growth of Smulekoff's. *Courtesy of the* Gazette.

The Braverman family had left western Europe in the 1890s and came to Cedar Rapids, where they created a legacy of excellent furniture stores. The youngest brother, Max Braverman, still in his teens, moved to Chicago to work in the furniture factories. Henry Smulekoff ran into Max during one of his buying trips in Chicago. Henry convinced eighteen-year-old Max to return to Cedar Rapids in 1900 and hired him as the bookkeeper for Smulekoff's Island Store. Soon, Max and his older brother Albert acquired Spokane Furniture at 223 Third Street SE, and in 1903, the two brothers opened the original People's Furniture on May's Island.

With the city actively buying up all of the properties on the island, Max and Albert closed Peoples in 1906 and opened Braverman's Furniture at 226 Second Street SE. A year later, they merged into the old Spokane Furniture location at 223 Third Street, keeping both the Braverman and the Spokane names alive. Max returned to Smulekoffs for a year before opening his own store, Max Furniture Store, in 1908, while continuing to assist in the operation of his brother Albert's store.

In 1913, Albert dropped the Braverman's business name and moved Spokane Furniture into the Fair complex at 210 First Avenue NE. Tiring of the furniture business, Albert turned the operation of the new store over to Mr. H.F. Paar and left town. Two years later, Mr. Paar purchased Spokane and renamed the store Paar Furniture Company, which in 1917, he changed again to Iowa Furniture.

Max Braverman continued operating Max Furniture for another twenty years. He closed it and shifted his energy toward purchasing and renting out apartments and business properties before his tragic death in 1932 at age fifty. The *Gazette*'s headline screamed, "BRAVERMAN DEATH SUICIDE." The next week, in a smaller article, it was corrected, saying the coroner found no evidence of suicide, just that a burner on the gas stove was left on while Max was at home eating his lunch, and he was overcome with the fumes and asphyxiated.

Hall-Ekfelt Furniture had locations in Waterloo and Ottumwa when it opened its new Cedar Rapids location in 1912, buying Romey-Welty Furniture at 220 First Avenue NE, located in the Fair. In 1914, Hall-Ekfelt moved to 216 Third Avenue SE. Fifteen years later, in 1929, the owners built and moved into a massive three-story building at 400 Third Avenue SE. By 1950, third-generation owner Hall A. Koontz was managing Hall-Ekfelt. This was its final downtown location before moving to 1618 Collins Road NE in April 1970 and changing the name to Hall Home Furnishings. It closed in 1991, and the Collins Road location later became a Rockwell Collins office.

DEPARTMENT STORES

Samuel G. Armstrong had a business philosophy he dedicated his life to: quality, personal service and selection. In 1890, when Mr. Armstrong was thirty-two years old, Armstrong, Fletcher & Co. opened at 120 Second Street SE. He started with just a forty-by-seventy-foot showroom and offered men's clothing and furnishings. In 1893, there was a change in ownership, and it became Armstrong, McClenahan & Co. The business grew and gradually expanded to three street addresses (120, 122 and 124) and sold its ware out of three floors and the basement. In 1913, the store was extended to the corner of Second Avenue. By 1920, the name was changed to Armstrong's Clothing, and the slogan, "Quality is Economy," was put to use. In 1928, Samuel died, and son Robert carried on the family business. In the early 1930s, it added Armstrong's Clothing for Women. By 1938, it had broadened its focus, advertising, "Quality is Economy—We are the Apparel Outfitters for the Entire Family—Men's, Women's, Boy's, Girl's and Babies. As well as Shoes, Millinery, Men's Hats, Furs, Sports Goods, and Home Furnishings."

In 1959, Armstrong's Department Store moved to 220 Third Avenue SE in the old Weller & Dows building, where it now had six floors of block-long display areas. Armstrong's had become one of the most popular stores in Cedar Rapids. The following are some fun quotes from various folks on the Cedar Rapids History Facebook page: "Shopped there all the time," "It was my favorite department store," "I purchased my wedding dress there," "I'd get on the bus and ride it downtown to Armstrong's" and "The air-door was so futuristic!"

By early 1990, Armstrong's was downsizing, and in late 1990, it closed for good.

Craemer's had downtown stores for seventy-eight years. It started in 1893 as Reps & Craemer's Dry Goods at 213 First Avenue SE. Today, this location is Coventry Gardens and Coventry Lofts. In 1896, the owners split up, and Reps Dry Goods carried on at that location until 1932. Meanwhile, Craemer's opened a dry goods store next door at 211 First Avenue SE in 1898, where it lasted until 1972, while also operating a second Craemer's location at 208 Second Avenue SE from 1937 to 1971.

The Fair was a masterful shopping mecca triumph. It took up the entire 200 block of First Avenue NE and delighted shoppers from 1903 to 1924. At first glance, it appeared to be one incredible gigantic block-long building with all retail storefronts. But this was actually an imposing series of identical three-story buildings anchored by the Franchere Department Store in the middle, another Waterhouse structure called the Merchants Block on the west end and the *Evening Gazette* building holding down the east end. This was the premier one-stop shopping destination of the day, offering furniture stores, grocery stores, clothing stores, wallpaper stores, jewelry stores, notion shops, a dentist and on and on. The Fair was demolished in 1925 to make way for the Roosevelt Hotel.

The Killian family had been in the retail business in Nebraska before coming to Cedar Rapids and opening a store in 1911 at 229 First Avenue and Third Street SE, which had previously been home to Taft's, and later

The Franchere Department Store, or the Fair, took up an entire block of First Avenue downtown. It was eventually replaced by the Roosevelt Hotel. *Courtesy of the History Center, Linn County Historical Society.*

Kresge's and, since 1971, has been the MNB corner parking lot. In 1913, Killian's relocated to its new five-story Fidelity Building at the corner of Third Avenue and Second Street, where the recently vacated city hall building (originally the Empire House hotel) had been. The new Killian's building took up an entire quarter of a city block, proclaiming in 1958, "Today we are 93 stores under one roof, all offering you a wider selection of merchandise than ever in our history." Killian's was an important downtown Cedar Rapids landmark for almost seventy years and closed in 1982.

Sears, Roebuck & Company opened its first Cedar Rapids location at 315 Third Avenue SE in 1928 in the old Kemble Floral shop. Needing more space, Sears expanded in 1945 and opened Sears Farm & Home Supply at 402 Second Avenue SE in the Poore Building, which had been home to several doctors, cafés and markets. In 1960, Sears closed both locations and moved to the new Lindale Plaza. The old Second Avenue building's second story was removed, and the building was dramatically remodeled and housed Downtown Tire Goodyear from 1962 to 2017. The building was scheduled to be torn down in 2018, but cooler heads prevailed, and it was saved and became the new location of Hazzard County, a country music bar that previously had been located in the old Dragon restaurant space for several years.

James Cash Penney opened a small shop in a small town in Wyoming in 1902. His success led to opening more locations, and by the time the Cedar Rapids' JC Penney opened in 1920, there were over 200 locations around the country. Noted as the fastest-growing department store in the country, by 1930, it had more than 1,500 locations. The first Cedar Rapids store was in the Delavan Hotel at 314 First Avenue NE on the first floor. Two years later, it moved across the street to 219 First Avenue SE. In 1926, it opened its 109 Second Street SE store, where it remained for over fifty years. In 1973, it opened an additional Cedar Rapids location, called the JC Penney Patio Store, in the Tycoon building at 427 Second Avenue SE. Both locations closed when Penney's became one of the founding anchors of Westdale Mall in 1979.

Montgomery Ward opened a Cedar Rapids location in 1933 in the Mullin Building at 219 Second Street SE. And forty-six years later, it also left downtown to become a founding anchor of Westdale. Wards closed the Westdale store in 2001, when the entire chain ceased operations.

FIVE-AND-DIME VARIETY STORES

Founded in 1878 in New York, the FW Woolworth Company was the original five-and-ten-cent store. The Woolworth's concept was quickly copied, and dime stores became a fixture in American downtowns. Fifty successful years later, Woolworths, looking for an edge over the competition, decided to eliminate its "price limits" strategy, and in 1935, Woolworths became a low-budget department store. The tactic worked, and by the Woolworth Company's 100th anniversary in 1978, it had become the largest department store chain in the world.

Woolworths came to Cedar Rapids in 1904 and offered its affordable goods to our citizens for more than eighty years. It changed locations several times, with two downtown stores open at the same time for several years and a store at Town & Country later in the '70s. Its last year in business in Cedar Rapids was 1986. Over the years they were located at 217 First Avenue SE (1904–17), 207 Second Avenue SE (1915–65), 210 Second Street SE (1917–23), 117 Second Street SE (1966–86).

SS Kresge's Five-and-Dime opened its first store in Memphis, Tennessee, in 1897. The variety store chain grew quickly and had eighty-five locations across the country before coming to Cedar Rapids in 1913. It opened for business at 229 First Avenue and Third Street SE, which was a Waterhouse Block corner structure. This three-story building had originally been home to CM Whitney Dry Goods in 1885, followed by Taft's Dry Goods from 1890 to 1910 and then the first local Killians location from 1911 to 1913. After eleven years, in 1924, the business was renamed Kresge's Five & Dollar. In 1950, the top two floors of the building were removed due to structural concerns. The Kresge organization rebranded several stores in 1965, including this one, which became Jupiter's Discount Store. It closed permanently in 1969, when the parent corporation opened Kmart West on Collins Road, which survived until 2012. The original downtown building was demolished and has been the MNB/Firstar/US Bank parking lot since 1971.

Neisner Brothers Five-and-Dime was located at 213 First Avenue SE in the old Reps Dry Goods building next to Craemer's. When it was preparing to open on December 1, 1934, ads in the *Cedar Rapids Tribune* announced, "Ready for business. 5 Cent to $1 Store. The public is cordially invited to look over the splendid merchandise the Neisner Brothers are offering to Cedar Rapids. A public inspection of the store will be held Friday, November 30, from 1:00 to 4:30 pm. WE ARE LOOKING FORWARD TO MEETING THE PEOPLE OF CEDAR RAPIDS."

The store was immediately popular and successful. Twenty-eight years later, Neisner's closed in 1962. Peoples Furniture moved in, offering fine furniture and home accessories, until it closed in 1974. The building then became a series of shops under the banner of Coventry Gardens, and in 2013, it was remodeled into housing spaces called Coventry Lofts.

The February 21, 1941 *Tribune* reported, "Clerks in Neisner Dime Stores Strike, Win Increases. Wage increases averaging $2.50 a week were won by employees of the Detroit area Neisner Bros ten-cent store here, after a strike lasting two months. Wages, which had been $12 to $13 a week for most of the girls, will be $15.50. Also agreed on is a scale of recognition of seniority in service. Clerks with one year of seniority are guaranteed 42 weeks of employment each year. The girls get vacations with pay, full pay for holidays, and time and a half when they work more than 48 hours a week."

CLOTHING STORES

Philadelphia Clothing Hall was located below the American House Hotel at Second Avenue and Second Street SE. The 1869 *Times* reported,

"Great attraction!!! Immense stock of clothing, which we are now selling at unusually low prices. Come Everybody! We have the goods, and are bound to sell them!" The Philadelphia Clothing Hall was open until 1874.

Golden Eagle Clothing opened in 1883 in the Craft Block on the corner of First Avenue and Second Street, with an address of 102 Second Street SE. It was the first store in town to use the newly available electric lights for illumination. It was a grand three-story redbrick building and still stands today. Golden Eagle closed in 1913. Later tenants included McClellan's Discount Store, Robinson's Store, Slumberland and AON. In the '60s, the façade was covered in aluminum panels, which have since been removed, and the brick finish restored. La Cantina Mexican Restaurant has been there since 2010.

Syndicate Clothing was a store for women at 207–209 First Avenue SE and operated from 1912 to 1964. It shared the building with The Bell, a "men's clothing and furnishings" store that opened for business in 1896 and was there until 1916. The next tenant was a S&H Green Stamps store. Later, part of the building was Gringo's Mexican Restaurant for many years, and then the Syndicate Epicurean Pub, named as a homage to the original ladies clothing store, was there from 2013 to 2016. The space has been vacated and remodeled and awaits its next tenant.

The building on the northeast corner of Second Avenue and Third Street was sometimes addressed as 122 Third Street SE and other times as 300 Second Avenue SE. First Baptist Church built a fine structure there in 1868, but as the downtown area grew and expanded and focused on business and retail, downtown churches found it beneficial to relocate elsewhere. By 1912, Cedar Rapids National Bank had built a two-story bank and office building on the site. The bank eventually merged with another bank and moved out, and in 1936, Jack Yager's Upstairs Store opened there. It was next door to Harmony Cafeteria on Third Street, and around the corner, on Second Avenue, was Probasco Jewelry and the Palace Theater. Yager's was a men's and boy's clothing store with the famous signage "We've Moved Up to Bring Prices Down" wrapped around the second-floor parapets. Yager's was in business almost twenty years and then closed in 1955. At that point, Kieck's, also a clothing store for men, moved in. Kieck's was only there for four years before moving out to Thirty-Second Street NE, where it operated for many decades. The old downtown corner of Second and Third is now the six-story US Bank parking ramp and the offices of Fusionfarm marketing services.

Distressingly, things downtown began changing in the 1950s. The department stores' commanding presence was dramatically affected by new concepts in retail: the idea of moving the stores closer to where the people lived. And smaller specialized shops started to make more sense than gigantic department stores. Shoppers liked the change—they had less distance to drive; the parking was easier, closer to the door and free; and they could select the store they wanted for the items they were looking for instead of wandering and browsing the aisles and the floors of the big department stores. Shopping shifted from an event to just go buy it and go home.

So, shopping centers were built. Lindale Plaza opened in 1960, taking Sears out of downtown. Westdale Mall opened in 1979, taking JC Penney and Montgomery Wards. Today, strip malls are all over town, although not downtown.

In 1956, the first mall in Iowa opened in Cedar Rapids. It was called Town & Country Shopping Center. It was a development of the Bucksbaum brothers from Marshalltown and was a successful venture that eventually evolved into General Growth Properties (GGP). Decades later, GGP built and operated Coral Ridge Mall in Coralville and the Jordan Creek Town Center shopping mall in Des Moines, as well as many other plazas and malls across the country.

Town & Country Shopping Center was erected in the 3600 and 3700 blocks of First Avenue SE, which had previously been open fields just north of Kenwood Park, which was the northern edge of Cedar Rapids at the time. It was huge—172,000 square feet of space in a big L-shaped building and parking for one thousand cars. May's Drug was on the south end next to First Avenue, and SunMart anchored the north end of the complex.

Over the years, the tenant lineup changed constantly, and sixty years later, this shopping center is still viable to shoppers and retailers.

The following is a partial list of businesses that have been located in Town & Country over the years: May's Drug, Sun Mart, Morris Plan, Kinney Shoes, Woolworths, Bremers, Toy Fair, Cedar Rapids Bowl, 300 Steak Lounge, Pfeiffer Jewelry, Globe Appliance, Duncan Photography, Lahr Paint, Lewellen Florist, Northwest Fabrics, So-Fro Fabrics, Pier 1 Imports, Grant's, Fanny Farmer, Baskin-Robbins, Ardan, Elaine Powers Figure Salon, Arnold Palmer Cleaners, Singer Sewing Machines, Flower City, Josef's Beauty Salon, Bankers Life, State Farm, Essen House, Randy's Restaurant, W.T. Grant, Kacere's, Famous Footwear, Chatty Kathy's, RJ Books Lounge, Rock N Bach Records, DeSoda's Nightclub, Borrowed

August 6, 1956 ad in the Cedar Rapids *Gazette* announcing the opening of the Town & Country Shopping Center, the first mall in Iowa. *Courtesy of the* Gazette.

Buck's Roadhouse, the Hub, Blarney Stone, Bridal Shop, Mercy Fitness Center, Antiques & Old Things, Sally's, Element Dance Club, 1st Avenue Live, Godfathers, Discount Eyeglasses and Rent-A-Center. And that's probably leaving out twenty more.

In 2014, the north section of the building was torn down, and a new Fareway grocery store was built and opened the following year.

PART VI

———— ✑ℓℓ ————

BUSINESSES

PIZZA JOINTS

You'd better cut the pizza in four pieces, because I'm not hungry enough to eat six.
—Yogi Berra

Who remembers growing up eating Chef Boyardee pizza on Saturday nights while watching the *Lawrence Welk Show* on the family black-and-white television? You made the dough from a mix, and the sauce was pretty awful, but still, there's just something about pizza. Americans first heard of the delicious pie from returning World War II soldiers who raved about the Italian delicacy.

The first mention of pizza in the *Cedar Rapids Gazette* was in 1945. It was a description of this unusual dish, along with a recipe, so you could try making it at home. Four years later, in 1949, the first advertisement appeared for a dining establishment offering pizza to its patrons.

The following are the first places that advertised the new Italian pizza pie, followed by additional notes and anecdotes of some of these places:

1949: Club 30, a roadhouse "outside the city limits" on Mount Vernon Road
1953: Louie Trombino's Roman Inn, in that same building
1953: Wendy Oaks Supper Club, one mile to the east, next door to the Lighthouse

1954: Ranch Supper Club, in Cou Falls on Highway 218, two miles past Swisher

1954: Naso's Pizza House, 1545 First Avenue SE, "the place that made pizza famous"

1955: Tony's Pizza Shop, 3334 First Avenue NE

1955: Leonardo's Pizza, Sixteenth Avenue SW at the Star Drive-In

1955: Old Hickory Inn, 4002 First Avenue NE, across from the Ford dealership

1956: Trombino's Pizzeria, in the old family home/grocery store at Seventeenth Avenue NE

1956: Colonial Restaurant, Sixteenth Avenue SW

1957: The first hearth-baked, fired-on-the-bricks pizza was introduced to Cedar Rapids at the Log Cabin on E Avenue NW.

Club 30

In 1949, the first place to sell pizza was on the outskirts of town. The main road leading into Cedar Rapids from the east was Highway 30, also called the Lincoln Highway and today known as Mount Vernon Road. Tourist camps and cafés welcomed travelers, and roadhouses sprang up. While the restaurants focused on serving meals, roadhouses thrived on the sale of beer and hard liquor, along with some food, and featured live music, dancing and sometimes gambling. Most roadhouses were located along highways and roads in rural areas, often on the outskirts, and it wasn't unusual for patrons to party into the early morning hours and, unfortunately for their neighbors, sometimes all night.

Truckers and travelers heading toward Cedar Rapids from the east would first notice the Midway Cafe about halfway between Mount Vernon and Cedar Rapids. Continuing west (and crossing Highway 151/13 which hadn't been built yet), next would be Wendy Oaks Super Club and the Lighthouse Inn on the left. A mile farther, the old Rosedale School was also on the left. After another mile, getting closer to town, on top of the hill on the right was the aptly named Hill Top Inn & Tavern, as well as the Wee Blue Inn, both established in the '30s and '40s.

At the southwest corner of the Lincoln Highway and Bertram Road intersection, the Rosedale School was a large two-story brick building under the jurisdiction of Bertram Township. One hundred or so students were split between the first-floor primary room for the younger kids and an upper room for the fifth, sixth, seventh and eighth graders. Graduates would move on to high schools in the Cedar Rapids city limits. According to newspaper reports, the Rosedale graduating class of '39 was the largest—eleven students graduated from eighth grade that spring. Rosedale closed for good in 1948, and all school-age rural kids were bussed into town.

The following year, Mitch Homsey opened a roadhouse in the old brick building. Mitch's Club 30 was a short-lived business with a colorful reputation. Originally open until 3:00 a.m., it was soon serving alcohol even later and promoting dancing and live music shows at 11:30 p.m., 1:30 a.m. and 3:30 a.m.

By May 1950, as the club was about to change hands, nearby residents were angry and frustrated with the havoc these places were creating. Complaints reported in the May 16 *Gazette* included screaming, fighting, all-night parties and that the roads near the businesses were littered with bottles and beer cans. Thirty-eight citizens met and, in a unanimous vote, asked the township trustees to revoke the permits of the Wee Blue Inn, Hill Top Inn and Club 30. It was noted that there had been no complaints lodged against the Lighthouse, Wendy Oaks or the Midway, which were regularly closed by 2:00 a.m.

Discussions among the residents, township trustees, Linn County sheriff, Linn County attorney and Linn County Board of Supervisors resulted in the immediate and permanent closing of Club 30 and the Hill Top Inn, with the Wee Blue Inn closing soon after.

By June, the Club 30/Rosedale building was listed for sale in *Gazette* classified ads. It reopened three years later, in 1953, as Louie Trombino's

Left: Club 30 ad in the July 3, 1949 Cedar Rapids *Gazette*. This is the first time a restaurant advertised pizza in the Cedar Rapids *Gazette*. *Courtesy of the* Gazette.

Right: Roman Inn took over the location of Club 30 and this was the second advertisement for pizza in the Cedar Rapids *Gazette*. *Courtesy of the* Gazette.

Roman Inn, which was open for only a short time. The old building was eventually torn down. In 1978, a beautiful new Knights of Columbus hall was built with a street address of 5977 Mount Vernon Road SE. After the Knights moved out in 2000, A Touch of Class event center took possession and is still operating twenty years later.

Leonardo's & Tony's

The Naso family has had a long history of providing food to the good people of Cedar Rapids. The family's patriarch, Anton "Tony" Naso Sr. was one of several Naso family members dealing in wholesale fruit products. As early as 1896, Tony Sr. sold fruit and groceries at his shop on First Avenue downtown in the far east storefront of the Fair retail complex.

By the early 1940s, his sons, Leo and Tony Jr., were operating Naso's Grocery on the west side of the river. In the middle of the decade, Tony Jr. left to join the army, after which he ended up in California, again in the grocery business. Meanwhile, Leo sold the west side grocery store and managed the Subway Bowling Alley in the basement of Guaranty Bank, which was later home to the Flame Room.

Tiring of the West Coast, Tony returned to Cedar Rapids in 1953 and joined Leo, who was now in the restaurant business at Park Court Lunch, 1545 First Avenue NE. They began having some success with the new product Tony brought with him: pizza. They renamed their restaurant Naso's Pizza House in 1954. Even though a few places beyond the city limits had pizza on their menus first, the Naso brothers will forever be known as the ones who introduced pizza to this city.

The potential for expanded pizza business was excellent, and the brothers immediately branched out. Leo went to the west side of town and started selling pizzas out of the Star Drive-In, eventually buying it and renaming it Leonardo's Pizza House. In 1965, he built a new building next door, and Leonardo's has been there ever since. Meanwhile, the old Star building became home to businesses such as Little Caesar's, Mike's Place and Domino's Pizza.

In 1955, Tony Naso left Naso's Pizza House and opened the first Tony's Pizza Shop & Deli at 3334 First Avenue NE. A year later, he moved up the block to 3300 First Avenue NE, which later became the Starlite Room. In 1957, Tony relocated his pizza business to 3334 First Avenue NE, which had previously been the old Dreme Drive-In/King's Drive-In. Finally, in 1969, when J&D Steakhouse took over that spot, Tony's new and final pizza joint was at 3847 First Avenue SE, where his business thrived for the next ten years. Winifred's has been operating at that location since 1983.

Earning the nickname "Cedar Rapids Pizza King," Tony Naso once estimated he'd sold 3.5 million pizzas in his lifetime.

Trombino's

The Trombino family had owned a grocery store in downtown Cedar Rapids, across from Greene Square Park, on the south side. In the 1930s, they operated a restaurant, Trombino's Roman Inn, at that same location, 525 Fourth Avenue SE. Years later, with new owners, that spot was home to Denny's Green Square Pub, followed by the Coopacabana.

In 1953, with the approval of the Bertram trustees, the board of supervisors and a zoning change, Louie opened the previously mentioned Louie Trombino's Roman Inn in the old Rosedale/Club 30 building. He was there for just a couple of years before relocating his pizza business to the family home at 1059 Seventeenth Street NE, which had been another Trombinos's Grocery location. He dropped the "Roman Inn" moniker, and Trombino's Pizzeria continued in operation from 1956 to 1964.

Colonial

The proprietors of the Old Hickory Inn were having great success on First Avenue NE in the late '50s and decided the time was right to open a second location on the west side of town. Situated on Sixteenth Avenue SW, next door to where the Howard Johnson Restaurant & Hotel would be built in the mid-1960s, was the Colonial Restaurant and Motel. The Colonial was in operation since 1954 and was the tenth place in

Colonial Restaurant was located at 2602 Sixteenth Avenue SW, later home to businesses such as Old Hickory West, Don & Al's Raceway, Fabs Fabric Center and Anytime Fitness. *Courtesy of the* Gazette.

Cedar Rapids that advertised pizza. Old Hickory West took over the location in 1960 and operated there the next four years. The site later became Al & Don's Family Raceway, a slot car racing venue, then Fabs Fabric Center and later Sports Liquidators. Most recently, it is Anytime Fitness.

Today

As pizza gradually took the country by storm, countless regional and national chains have been popular: Shakey's, Happy Joe's, Pizza Ranch, Godfather's and Chuck E. Cheese, to name a few. Some businesses offer only take-out pizza, like Casey's General Store and Papa Murphy's. Others offer only home delivery, such as Papa John's, Little Caesars, Domino's, Pizza Hut and Paul Revere's, which was founded in Cedar Rapids. As a matter of fact, in 2001, the Paul Revere's location in Mt. Pleasant, Iowa, set a Guinness world record for the largest commercially available pizza. For only $99.99, you could get the Ultimate Party Pizza, which measured four feet in diameter, and they'd deliver it to your door.

Who has a frozen pizza in their freezer at home right now? Popular brands include Jacks, Tony's, Red Baron, Tombstone and Totinos, with DiGiorno being the highest-selling frozen pizza in the United States today. If you prefer to go out for a pizza pie, Cedar Rapidians rave about Tomaso's, Zoey's, Mr. B's for Sam's Pizza or Miguel's in the old Pizza Inn building. And that is just a partial list.

Today, sixty-five years after helping introduce pizza to the Cedar Rapids area, Leonardo's and Naso's are still at it, providing tasty pizza pies to hungry folks.

MOTORCYCLE DEALERS

You are on your own. You are not protected by two tons of steel, rubber, foam padding and safety glass. Neither are you steering two tons of guided missile toward other cars, people and property. If you are prepared to accept the responsibility of your own actions, then motorcycling can be both safe and thrilling. Riding is an art as well as a craft and no amount of explanation can take the place of experience.
—Theresa Wallach, Easy Motorcycle Riding, 1970

The passion for riding motorcycles shows up in many popular sayings today: Let's ride; get some wind; experience the freedom of riding on two wheels; four wheels move your body, but two wheels move your soul; "I don't really feel like going for a ride today," said no motorcycle rider ever; born to be wild.

These are mantras that are repeated across the world, and Cedar Rapids is no exception. The lengthy list of dealers who set up shop to sell new motorcycles in Cedar Rapids over the years proves this point. Harley, Indian, Honda, Yamaha, Suzuki, Kawasaki, BMW and more have all been represented by local dealerships. The following is a partial list that paints a clear picture of the area's interest in motorcycling:

HARLEY-DAVIDSON
2415 Westdale Drive SW; Metro; Rick Bowman (2002–present)
1846 Sixteenth Avenue SW; Rick Bowman; 1984 Suzuki; added Harley from 1988–2002
1810 Highway 965 North Liberty; Bernie Huber (1977–93)
1507 C Street SW; Bernie Huber (1968–72)
620 Center Point Road NE; Wilson's Motorcycle (1956–68)
724 Third Street SE; Mike Wilson (1954)
510 Third Avenue SE; Morgan Brothers (1940–50)

INDIAN
A-1 Performance Powersports at 6969 Mount Vernon Road SE (2013–present)
Indian Motorcycles (2011–13)
LaDage Indian Motorcycle Shop at 325 First Street SW (1950)
Cliff's Indian Shop (1940)
West Side Motorcycle Club (1919)

METRIC
McGrath Powersports at 4645 Center Point Road NE (2015–present)
Metro Motorsports at 2415 Westdale Drive SW; Rick Bowman (2002–present)
5 Seasons Motorsports at 506 North Center Point Road, Hiawatha; Bill Bennett (2002–05)
CR Honda Yamaha at 5711 Sixteenth Avenue SW (1993)
Pazour Motor Sports at 2021 Sixteenth Avenue SW; Bob Pazour (1993)
Pazour Motor Sports at 3303 Sixteenth Avenue SW (1968–87)
Cedar Rapids Yamaha (1988–90)
Pazour Motor Sports (1968–87)

Harley-Davidson at 1507 C Street SW; Bernie Huber (1968–72)
    Pazour Cycle Co.; Bob Pazour (1967)
    Pazour Cycle Co. at 1918 C Street SW; in his mom's garage (1954–56)

OTHER
G.A. Sayers Motorcycles at 324 Third Street SE (1920s)
Smulekoff Motorcycles & Bicycles at 129 First Street SE (1912)

Kapa Ann *Riverboat*

*Dancin' in the moonlight, everybody's feelin' warm and bright, it's such a fine and
natural sight, everybody's dancin' in the moonlight.*
    —*Van Morrison/King Harvest*

The Cedar River was originally an important source of power generation
and provided an efficient way to move products, grain and other goods to
and from the city. And our citizens have long taken advantage of the river's
recreational benefits. In 1842, the visiting steamboat *Maid of Iowa* chugged
into town and offered excursions to the city's residents.

After 111 years, we had our own pleasure vessel. The *Kapa Ann* was a
combination excursion boat, riverboat and dance boat that was built and
operated in Cedar Rapids by Paul and Ann Miller. The boat's name was
devised from the first letters of their names, beginning with their daughter
Kathy's name.

Cruises began in July 1953. The boat was moored near Ellis Park, and
Coonrod was hired to pull it onto the bank during the winter and push it
back into the river each summer. It could carry up to 150 passengers and
was piloted by Dennis Murphy.

It had a completely enclosed cedar superstructure with a thick steel hull
and was powered by two big Chris-Craft one hundred horsepower six-
cylinder marine engines. The boat was twenty-four feet wide by sixty-four
feet long, weighed twenty-six tons and had an onboard generator to power
the lights and electric devices.

Technically a floating ballroom, the *Kapa Ann* had a thirteen-by-forty-four-
foot hardwood dance floor in the center, booths on the sides, coolers for pop
and ice cream and a Wurlitzer jukebox.

Hour-long cruises were available on Sunday afternoons for thirty-five
cents per passenger. Two-hour cruises were offered on Friday, Saturday and

Sunday nights, costing seventy-five cents per passenger. Private parties could book the boat from Monday through Thursday.

The *Kapa Ann* was sold in 1967 and subsequently changed hands several times, continuing to operate on the Cedar through the '70s. In 1977, it was moved overland to Dubuque and was remodeled into a houseboat. It floated for the next decade and was eventually pulled onto dry land and converted to a cabin. Today, it sits on the shore of Mid-Town Marina in East Dubuque, Illinois.

MOTEL SEPIA

White travelers have no idea of how much nerve and courage it requires for a Negro to drive coast to coast in America. He achieved it with nerve, courage, and a great deal of luck, supplemented by a road atlas, and the Green Book travel guide, a listing of places in America where Negroes can stay without being embarrassed, insulted, or worse.
—*John Williams,* This Is My Country Too, *1965*

Cecil Reed, born in 1913 in Illinois, moved with his family to Cedar Rapids in 1923 when his father got a job as a custodian at the Union Station. Cecil attended school, worked odd jobs and married Evelyn Collins at age twenty. They both stayed steadily employed, saved money, bought a home and raised four kids. In 1944, Cecil started a business with his brothers called Reed's Floor Care.

In 1950, Cecil and Evelyn bought a small piece of property along Mount Vernon Road SE, at the southeast corner of the intersection with Bertram Road, which was considered "out in the country" at that time. Just to the west, across Bertram Road, a building was built that later that housed the Knights of Columbus hall, now A Touch of Class event center. About three-quarters of a mile farther east was the popular Lighthouse Inn.

The Reeds lived in a house on the property and built a structure to house the floor care business. They also cleared the rest of the property of brush and developed a kid's park and eventually a small racetrack for quarter midget cars. They also took a long cross-country trip that changed their lives.

During their road trip across America, they struggled to find overnight lodging because of their skin color, which was not an uncommon occurrence during the segregated 1940s and '50s. Before the legislative accomplishments of the civil rights movement, simple auto journeys for black people were fraught with difficulty and potential danger. Black travelers were often barred from restaurants and bathrooms, but finding accommodations was one of the greatest challenges. They often had to spend hours in the evening trying to find somewhere to stop, sometimes resorting to sleeping in haylofts or their own cars if they could not find lodging anywhere.

On their return to Cedar Rapids, Cecil and Evelyn began remodeling the building that housed their floor care business. Naming it Motel Sepia, they intended to offer lodging to African American travelers. It opened in 1953, and the motel gradually grew to ten units, and they soon accepted guests of all races. At that time, that stretch of Mount Vernon Road was Highway 30, the designated Lincoln Highway route. Traffic was busy, with tourists passing by constantly.

In those days, there was a guidebook available for black travelers, called *The Green Book*. It was considered "the Bible of black travel during Jim Crow" and enabled black travelers to find lodgings, businesses and gas stations that would serve them. Motel Sepia was one of the highly recommended places in the guidebook.

By the '60s, business had slowed, and the Reeds sold the property and moved into town. Cecil became active in politics, ran for office, served as state legislator and then held other various government positions. All of the Motel Sepia buildings were removed when the Highway 30 roadway was widened and raised, and the area is now overgrown with brush and trees.

DANIELS PARK FOODS

When I was a kid, my uncle had a grocery store. I still remember the smell of sawdust on the floor.
—Frankie Avalon

Oakland Road was the original route from Cedar Rapids to Marion, long before the Marion Boulevard (now called First Avenue) was built. In fact, if you follow Oakland Road north from the Center Point Road intersection behind Coe College, after about twenty blocks, you'll notice the name changes to Old Marion Road. It originally continued diagonally past KGAN/FOX (formerly the WMT studios) and Collins Road and then headed straight north on what is now C Avenue, then jogged east to

Twixt Town Road, finally crossing Indian Creek near Thomas Park and the McDonalds.

But back on Oakland, three blocks ahead of the Oakland/Center Point Road intersection, is a historic building. Located at 901 Oakland Road NE is the old Daniels Park Food store, which is now home to Kevin's A-1 vacuum cleaner sales and service. The following is a list of business occupants from years past:

Indra's Grocery: John F. and Stella Indra (1913–39)
Daniels Park Foods: Charles and Lillian Krejci (1940–82)
Daniels Park Grocery: Connie O'Connell (1982–86)
Daniels Park Pohlena Foods (1986)
Nemer's Grocery: Everett and Karen Nemer (1987)
Curl's Upholstery & Furniture (1989–98)
Cedar Valley Sports (2000–04)
Cedar Rapids Bridge Studio (2008)
Kevin's A-1 Vacuum (2014–present)

If you're familiar with the area, you've probably heard of, and maybe even shopped at, the old corner grocery store Daniels Park Foods. It was immensely popular for its meats—slabs would come in at the back, and ceiling-mounted racks let them move it around the room for cutting. A huge meat locker took up a large portion of the space.

But the story of the original owners, the Indras, is quite interesting. Their story starts in Europe.

John Indra was born in 1840 in Moravia, a region that later became part of Czechoslovakia. In 1869, at age twenty-nine, he immigrated to the United States and ended up in Cedar Rapids. He and his wife, Josephine, had two children, a boy and a girl. Their son, John F. Indra, was born in 1877. Prior to 1884, there was no one with the surname "Indra" listed in the city directories. They were likely renting a room or living with relatives. John Indra made his first appearance in the Cedar Rapids City Directory in 1884.

John was a laborer at the BCR&N railroad shops, and the Indras lived at 340 B Avenue NE. By 1895, at age fifty-five, John Indra had changed careers and was now listed as a clerk at Central Park Grocery, located at 1202 B Avenue NE, where the Indra family now lived.

The residential district surrounding Coe College was nicknamed Central Park at that time. Later, when the college needed the Indra's property for expansion, the family moved a couple of blocks north. Meanwhile, with new owners, Central Park Grocery moved to 1600 E Avenue NE. Next door to the new location, in the same building at 1602 E Avenue, was the Central Park Tavern, known as Chyba's Tavern in the '50s and '60s, Werni's Tap in the '70s and '80s, Mahoney's from the late '90s to the mid-2010s and then Dick's Tap & Shakeroom for a bit. Today it is MOCO Hot Dog Bar.

After vacating the B Avenue location, John and Josephine and their two adult children lived at 1301 D Avenue NE. By 1900, the elder Indras owned a grocery store around the corner at 418 Thirteenth Street NE. The 1901 directory shows that twenty-four-year-old John F. Indra was working there too. That section of Thirteenth Street NE is better known as Center Point Road, and the first three-block section off First Avenue, which goes through the center of campus, is actually named College Drive. Today, that Indra Grocery property is taken up by Coe College's Clark Racquet Center.

In late 1903, Josephine passed away. John sold the store to his son, and despondent over his wife's death, he took his own life a few months later at age sixty-four. The headline in the *Republican* said, "Suicide—Grocer Indra Swallows Acid."

In 1906, John F. and his wife, Stella, were still running the grocery store on Thirteenth Street/Center Point Road and were living there. By 1910, John F. and Stella had sold the store and moved, and he had taken another job at Reps Dry Goods store, which was downtown on First Avenue next door to Craemer's. A year later, in 1911, John F. was at another new job at Frick-Stearns-Russell Co., a successful wholesale grocer. But at age thirty-five, John F. Indra was compelled to once again own a neighborhood grocery store.

A few blocks northwest of Coe College in a thinly settled part of town was a vacant tract of land at 901 Oakland Avenue NE, directly across the street from Daniels Park. There was nothing there before 1913, which was the year Indra's Grocery opened. John F. and Stella Indra built the two-story building, lived above the store and raised a family there. John and Stella had three sons and five daughters, and by the early 1930s, four of the now-adult Indra children appeared in the directories, all living at the 901 address. The Indras bought the two houses next door on Oakland and eventually tore down the little house at 903 to make room for a parking lot.

The Indras proudly operated their new grocery store for twenty-four years, until they sold it to Charles and Lillian Kejci, who took over in 1939. The Krejcis renamed it Daniels Park Foods and expanded the meat-cutting part of the business.

DANIELS PARK FOODS was established more than 30 years ago, at its present location, which was then a thinly settled district of Cedar Rapids. The original founder was John F. Indra, who operated the business until 1939, when the present owners, Charles and Lillian Krejci purchased the store.

Daniels Park Foods today offers a complete line of choice meats, fresh fruits and vegetables, and high quality grocery items. Courteous service to their customers is the policy. Prompt delivery service, too, will make shopping for your grocery needs a pleasure at Daniels Park Foods.

We join with you in congratulating Iowa on her Centennial Anniversary.

FOR A CHOICE SELECTION OF:

★ QUALITY MEATS

★ FRESH FRUITS AND VEGETABLES

★ CANNED GOODS AND SUNDRIES

GET ACQUAINTED WITH
DANIELS PARK FOODS!

LOOK FOR AN IMPORTANT ANNOUNCEMENT . . .
Which We Will Make Very Soon!

DANIELS PARK FOODS

901 OAKLAND ROAD NE.

Daily Deliveries Except Wednesday. Orders Received by 12 Noon
Delivered Same Day. Minimum Order $1.50 For Delivery.

Above: Daniels Park Foods building in 2020. *Photo by Peter D. Looney.*

Left: Daniels Park Foods promotion in the August 11, 1946 Cedar Rapids *Gazette. Courtesy of the* Gazette.

Now in their sixties, John F. and Stella moved into the house across the parking lot, at 915 Oakland Avenue. John F. Indra died in 1952 at age seventy-five. Their sons had found jobs in town, and the girls had married and acquired new last names, Wiggins, Hoyt, Janda and Dvorak, and raised their own families. The last year any Indras are listed in the Cedar Rapids City Directory is 1971.

STAR WAGON COMPANY

Now that the manufacture of Star Wagons has become one of the leading industries of the City, and the favorite wagon of the West, it will be seen that nearly if not quite absolute perfection has been attained in the manufacture of the Star Wagon.
—Cedar Rapids Times, *April 24, 1873*

A local manufacturer began producing farm and lumber wagons in Cedar Rapids in 1866. Upton, Chambers & Company built its factory on the north end of town, near what was eventually the Quaker Oats property. Its product brand name was Star Wagons. The vehicles were sturdy and reliable, and the company grew.

In 1871, the business was officially incorporated, and the name was changed from Upton, Chambers, & Company to the Star Wagon Company, with George Greene as president. That same year, the factory suffered a devastating fire and burned to the ground.

Greene decide to rebuild the company on the south side of town in the quickly growing Fourth Street rail corridor. He purchased property between Twelfth and Thirteenth Avenues SE, which years later, became the site of Iowa Steel and Iron companies.

The new facility was completed in 1872. The company picked up where it left off, and by 1877, it was producing more than three thousand vehicles per year and had become one of Cedar Rapids' largest employers. In another couple of years, the enterprise was recognized nationally as one of the leading wagon builders.

In *Wheels that Won the West*, David Sneed states, "While Star Wagon was never the powerhouse of manufacturing that Studebaker and others were, they were clearly far from being a marginal bystander. During their startup in 1866, vehicle offerings were limited to lumber and farm wagons. By

Star Wagon Company was a leading wagon manufacturer and a leading area employer.
Courtesy of the History Center, Linn County Historical Society.

the 1880s their product line had greatly expanded to also include drays, ice wagons, heavy trucks, butcher's wagons, milk wagons, express wagons, ranch wagons, oil wagons, grain wagons, furniture wagons, road wagons, road carts, surreys, phaetons, bob sleds, and numerous styles of carriages."

Star Wagon's business began to decline as orders fell off during the 1890s. Like so many other firms, the economic depression created by the Panic of 1893 likely added to the swift downfall of this business. By 1900, the Star Wagon Company was no longer in business.

LOG CABIN TOURIST CAMP/TWIN TOWERS

Listed AAA Camp—20 Cabins Furnished with Linen, Bedding, Running Water, Gas Plates and Electricity—and a Children's Playground.
—1933 Cedar Rapids Phonebook

Travelers passing through town needed a place to stop for the night. From the 1920s through the '50s, cabin camps were popular because they were right on the highways at the outskirts of towns. Before high-speed, four-lane interstates were common, the Lincoln Highway was the busiest road through

Cedar Rapids. On the east side, where it followed Highway 30 and Mount Vernon Road SE, there were four camps: the Lighthouse Cabins behind the Lighthouse Inn; Kozy Korner Trailer Kamp at 3138 Mount Vernon Road, Evening Star Tourist Camp and the Lincolnway Court Cabins, where All Saints Elementary Catholic School is now.

On the western edge of town, where the Lincoln Highway followed Highway 30 and Johnson Avenue NW, the Log Cabin Tourist Camp opened in 1927. Before then, the area had been farmland, timber and streams. Owners John and Anna Cox lived in a two-story house on the north side of the highway, which served as the office, with the cabins situated right behind them.

In 1929, the Coxes built the Twin Tower Cafe next door, directly to the west of their house, to further accommodate travelers. The Twin Towers building had two distinctive towers at both front corners of the structure.

As highway traffic increased, the property was enlarged to include gas pumps, additional parking and vehicle service and was called the Twin Towers Cafe & Truck Stop. From 1930 to 1939, you could fill up the tank, grab a bite, take a break from your journey and spend the night if you liked.

In 1940, the designated highway was rerouted a few miles to the south, now following Sixteenth Avenue SW. So, the enterprising owners of the Twin Towers moved their operation to the southwest corner of the intersection of Sixteenth Avenue and Williams Boulevard SW. Again, cabins, a restaurant and a service station were built.

The business ran its course for thirty years, and by 1972, the Twin Towers had closed. The property was cleared, and Eagle Foods built a large store on the site. In the late '80s, Western Auto took over the building, followed by Advanced Auto Parts. Recently, Cassill Motors moved to that busy corner.

Just a half-mile west on Sixteenth Avenue had been another smaller stop for weary travelers and hungry diners. E&R Motel and Cafe operated at the southwest corner of Sixteenth Avenue and Edgewood Road SW from 1947 to 1969. That location was later home to Mr. Steak, Bonanza and Happy Joe's. Today, the site is a CVS Pharmacy.

Meanwhile, on Johnson Avenue, after the Coxes moved to Sixteenth Avenue, the original Twin Towers building was remodeled into New Castle Apartments. The two-story house/camp office was eventually home to the Sampson family, where radio legend and fellow local historian Rick Sampson grew up. Both buildings are still standing and viable to this day.

THE LITTLE GALLERY

When artists give form to revelation, their art can advance, deepen and potentially transform the consciousness of their community.
—Alex Grey

The only time I feel alive is when I'm painting.
—Vincent Van Gogh

Maybe in our world, there lives a happy little tree over there.
—Bob Ross

This final profile is not really about a business; instead, it's about the business of displaying works of art for an appreciative public. Cedar Rapids has always taken pride in promoting the importance of books and literature, and their words and stories are interwoven with the importance of art. It's a winding story.

There's long been a quiet cultural district in Cedar Rapids, located in the 800 block between First and Second Avenues SE. It includes the Grant Wood Studio; the Masonic Grand Lodge, Library and Museum; the Douglas Mansion, now the History Center; and in the 1930s, the Little Gallery.

The story begins in 1884, when the Masonic Library opened to the public at 813 First Avenue SE. Books and artifacts were displayed, and the property and buildings were enlarged, eventually replaced by the white marble Grand Lodge and Masonic Library building.

In 1895, community leaders and artists had returned to town after a trip to Chicago to see a major art exhibition and formed the Cedar Rapids Art Club. Meanwhile, the Douglas Mansion was being built at 800 Second Avenue SE. George Bruce Douglas and his wife, Irene, had promoted and supported arts in the city. Eventually, the Douglases swapped homes with Caroline Sinclair and moved to her property, renaming it Brucemore. Mrs. Sinclair's family occupied the 1897 Douglas Mansion until 1923.

The new Cedar Rapids Carnegie Library had opened in 1905 on Third Street SE. The library offered a specially designed gallery on the second floor to the Art Club, which moved in and soon incorporated as the Cedar Rapids Art Association and began exhibiting art created by locals. The first painting was acquired for the collection in 1906. Paintings and sculptures were on display, and highly respected annual exhibitions were offered. By the early 1920s, artists Grant Wood and Marvin Cone were among the most active members.

In 1924, the Turner family acquired the Douglas/Sinclair property and converted it into Turner Mortuary East. The family hired Grant Wood to decorate and furnish the interior and design the landscaping of the grounds. Grant Wood was also offered use of the detached carriage garage as living quarters and a studio. He remodeled it and lived there until the mid-1930s, doing some of his most important paintings during his time there, including *American Gothic*.

In 1928, the Cedar Rapids Art Association received financial support from both the American Federation of Arts and the Carnegie Foundation and opened the Little Gallery at 318 Third Street SE. The Coe College student newspaper, *the Cosmos*, stated on October 11, 1928, "The Little Gallery is an experiment that is attracting attention throughout the country. By means of this, an art gallery with a focus on local artists has only graced cities much larger than Cedar Rapids. Exhibitions that are shown here compare favorably with those of New York and Chicago. The people who have been put in charge are authorities in their fields. It is no unpleasant duty to visit such galleries and exhibitions as ours."

The mission of the gallery was not only to display paintings, sculptures and other works of art but also to promote art awareness and education in the community. The gallery was directed by Edward Rowan, a sculptor, painter and educator, who later helped run the national Public Works of Art Project.

In 1931, the Little Gallery relocated to a magnificent two-story house at 839 First Avenue SE, on the property directly east of the Masonic Library. The house was a gift donated by Mrs. Austin Palmer. The structure was redesigned with a reception hall, exhibition halls, a children's room, space for classes in cooperation with the Coe College art department and space for the Little Gallery Junior Art Club. There was an elaborate black wood and wrought-iron stairway and railing leading to the second floor, which itself was a work of art.

Various art was displayed, including not only paintings and sculptures but also photography, crafts, embossed leather, jewelry, published works, hand-bound books and manuscripts. The grand opening was on November 1, 1931. Advertisements stated, "No invitations have been mailed, in an effort to carry out the democratic policy that the gallery and the opportunities it offers belong to the people of Cedar Rapids. It is open to all."

But the Great Depression soon affected the gallery. Funds for art disappeared, the property was sold and the Little Gallery moved back into the Carnegie Library in 1935.

In 1966, the Cedar Rapids Art Association found space in the Torch Press Building at 324 Third Street SE. Renamed the Cedar Rapids Art Center, sixteen thousand square feet were renovated over four floors, and artwork was once again displayed. By the mid-1980s, the Cedar Rapids Public Library had moved to a new location on First Street, vacating the Carnegie building where the Art Association had first been established. The City of Cedar Rapids offered the building and adjacent property to the Art Center. The new Cedar Rapids Museum of Art was formally opened in 1989 and is still there today.

In 2002, the building that housed the original studio of Grant Wood, known by its fictitious address of 5 Turner Alley, opened for tours. And in 2018, the History Center moved into the old Douglas Mansion, completing the circle. The Masonic Library and Museum, the History Center and the Grant Wood Studio have returned the 800 block to a cultural area.

CONCLUSION

There are more Cedar Rapids businesses and buildings and landmarks that are lost—a lot more. People have memories of many more places. More information is out there that needs to be collected and shared and passed on. I'm headed back to the old phone books and directories and newspapers so that we can feel confident about the accuracy of the names and dates and places.

Meanwhile, the world keeps spinning, time keeps passing, things keep changing. Old buildings will get torn down, and new buildings will go up. Buildings aren't built to last forever. I don't whine about that—I'm OK with that. I get it. I'm OK with progress. It is what it is. So, I will keep collecting the old pictures I come across and keep taking pictures of old buildings. I will keep documenting what I can find and keep sharing information about lost landmarks.

And one more thing: thank you for your interest in local history.

BIBLIOGRAPHY

Clements, Ralph. *Tales of the Town*. Cedar Rapids, IA: Stamats Publishing Company, 1967.

Danek, Ernie. *Cedar Rapids, Tall Corn and High Technology*. Woodland Hills, CA: Windsor Publications, 1980.

Henry, George T., and Mark W. Hunter. *Then & Now: Cedar Rapids*. Charleston, SC: Arcadia Publishing, 2003.

"Our People, Our Story." *Cedar Rapids Gazette*, 2004.

Smith, Sue Davis, and Bernard Smith and Neil Baumhover. *Cedar Rapids: Prologue & Promise*. Cedar Rapids, IA: WDG Communications, 1998.

Strong, Jean. *The Marion Library: Doorway to the Future*. North Liberty, IA: Ice Cube Press, 2005.

Svendsen, Marlys. *Historical and Architectural Reconnaissance Survey Report for the Downtown and Industrial Corridors in Cedar Rapids, Iowa*. Sarona, WI: Svendsen Tyler, 1997.

Special thanks to the Cedar Rapids Public Library's Digital Archives for offering online access to publications, such as Cedar Rapids phonebooks, city directories and various Cedar Rapids newspapers.

INDEX

T

Time Check 101, 102
Times Theater 30, 42, 45
Town Theater 26, 70
train depots 117, 118, 119, 149

W

World Playhouse 36, 37, 42

Y

YMCA 31, 67, 138, 139, 140,
      143, 144
YWCA 67, 138, 140, 141

ABOUT THE AUTHOR

Peter D. Looney is a life-long Iowan who grew up on a small farm near the small town of Solon, situated between Cedar Rapids and Iowa City. Due to his passion for rock music, the bulk of his past writing has involved the eastern Iowa music scene, where he has profiled over one hundred local bands for the *Cedar Rapids Gazette*'s *Hoopla* magazine. His fascination with local history led to extensive probing of the area's past music venues and clubs, which led to his collection of photographs and stories of almost every other "lost" business and landmark in the area.